MW01286888

Coaching Middle School Cross Country and Track & Field

Practical Guidance and Sample Workouts for Beginner Coaches

Timothy Rayle, Ph.D.

To the athletes past, present and future who were provided a spark by an amazing coach. To the coaches who, likewise, were provided a spark by remarkable athletes.

CONTENTS

FOREWORD

Coaching adolescent cross country and track athletes provides many challenges and appears to be one of the most complex times to influence athletes. Among those challenges are extreme emotional and physiological development, which is already taking place independently from any sport-specific training the student might attempt. Often times, helping athletes through this confusing stage of their life can carry tremendous importance. Coaches in this environment wouldn't be surprised to find that they carry an important role in the life of their athletes; a role that might ultimately be bigger than just "coach".

Showing athletes at any age, but especially the middle school age, that you care for them and will give them appropriate training to improve their abilities and avoid getting them hurt will have an incredibly endearing effect.

Dr. Rayle has addressed these difficult concepts in an organized way in *Coaching Middle School Cross Country and Track and Field, Practical Guidance and Sample Workouts for Beginner Coaches*. His thorough yet simple presentation could lead anyone from their first day on the job, to writing end-of-season workouts, all while keeping the interest of the athlete in the forefront. As a former athlete of his, and product of his work, I am confident that his material can help develop further coaches of successful athletes.

– Josh Wolfe, Head Cross Country and Assistant Track & Field Coach, Indiana Tech

ACKNOWLEDGMENTS

To Julie Rayle and Ginger Rayle, who inspire and encourage me to use the gifts God has given me to provide opportunities for others.

To the athletes I have been blessed with coaching, thank you for the memories, for making training and competing enjoyable, and especially for providing affirmation that a coach's approach makes all the difference in the world.

To Julie Rayle, Aaron Slater, Mandy Slater, Greg Wolf, and Josh Wolfe, thank you for your content and editing suggestions.

To Josh Wolfe, who is an outstanding cross country and track & field coach, thank you for your comprehensive training advice and your willingness to assist athletes and coaches at every level.

1

QUALITY COACHES AT THE MIDDLE SCHOOL LEVEL

Who in their right mind signs up for the opportunity to coach middle school cross country or track and field? The answer is individuals who have a desire to work with children during the most influential time of their young lives.

In many middle schools, you will find three categories of coaches: (1) Those who are more than happy to work with this age group but who know very little to nothing about the sports; (2) Those who are overzealous believing they know pretty much everything about the sports and overemphasize winning as the ultimate goal. These individuals also promote the idea that only the top performing athletes should have the privilege of competing; (3) Those who know the sports, have a deep understanding of middle school students, and want to make a positive difference in the lives of all middle school athletes. I call this group the quality coaches.

Coaches in the first group, if willing to learn the

basics, move into group three, and become inspirations for the athletes. The parents of the children these coaches work with encourage other parents to have their children join the team. These coaches predictably have record numbers of athletes join the teams they are coaching.

Coaches in the second group, even though they often present themselves as being very charismatic, are less inspirational; they create turmoil and cause a decrease in the number of athletes joining the team. This is because the athletes very quickly become aware of the coach's tactics of only paying positive attention to the top performing athletes.

The third group is a rarity at the middle school level since they are in high demand and their expertise can be adapted to the high school and post-high school levels. These coaches have an outstanding rapport with all athletes, parents, other coaches, and officials. Student-athletes flock to these coaches because there is mutual respect and the athletes know the coach is looking out for their best interests.

Since you are reading this book, there's a high probability you are either in group one or group three. If you happen to be a member of group two, there's still hope for you and the athletes you coach as you continue reading the following pages and then applying the information to your coaching technique.

Understanding Needs of Athletes

Middle school students are experiencing the world differently than they did as elementary students. For many students, this is the first time they are thrown into different social situations based upon their class schedules and their before-school and after-school activities. They could experience five, six, seven, or more different social situations per day.

In the primary grades, students focused on meeting their basic needs – security, safety, food, water, etc. Now, in middle school, the priority is belongingness and esteem needs. Understand that during the middle school years intimate relationships, friends, and feelings of accomplishment take center stage.

When many think of middle school athletes, the emphasis usually is placed on the physical, social, and emotional self-consciousness that manages to accompany children at this age. Even though many middle school students do not have the physiques we associate with top performing athletes, this should not concern you. As a coach of middle school athletes, the primary focus of your coaching must be on the full participation and skill refinement of each child on your team, regardless of your perception of their athletic ability. You as the coach have the awesome opportunity to make a positive impact on the athletic, social, and emotional development of every middle school child who comes out for your team by allowing the athlete, regardless of current ability or body type, the expectation of practicing and competing.

This is where the importance of having quality coaches at the middle school level is of primary significance. A quality coach is able to maintain the parameters within the team which allow all the athletes, regardless of ability level, to feel accepted, to feel competent, and to experience a sense of achievement. Although winning is enjoyable, quality coaches do not place winning as the primary objective, but rather see it as an outcome of skill development.

Quality Characteristics

How does one become a quality coach? It's actually a straightforward process. Focus on developing in yourself the characteristics or traits every child desires in an adult role model. So then, what are these characteristics or traits?

Quality coaches:

- Focus on full athletic participation and skill refinement.
- Make sure every athlete feels welcome and special.
- Take time to be educated about the sport.
- Establish rapport with the athletes, parents, and families.
- Facilitate the learning process.
- Are enthusiastic and encouraging.
- Are inspirational.
- Are organized.
- Are committed to the school community.
- Are character builders.
- Are patient.
- Are ethical.
- Are gracious.
- Make the sport fun.
- Develop leadership traits.
- Are consistent.
- Seek help and improvement.
- Are compassionate.

- Are empathetic.
- Delegate responsibility.
- Communicate.
- Are positive.
- Are creative.

Finding a Quality Mentor

Experience is the greatest teacher when it comes to developing into a quality coach. One of the strongest recommended ways to gain insight and valuable know-how is through interaction with a mentor who exhibits the quality coaching traits. Whether it be an expert who is located locally or across the state, nation, or world, it's highly advisable to reach out to him/her. When it comes to cross country and track and field coaches, these coaches are totally focused on helping all athletes reach success, regardless of whose team the athlete is on. Similarly, when you reach out for help in understanding how to be successful, you will be hard-pressed to meet a productive cross country and/or track coach who is not willing to mentor other coaches.

When looking for a mentor, it is important to look at the coach's total program. If he/she has a strong program year after year with many beginner, intermediate and established athletes, and also a robust parent base with the team, he/she is a good coach to learn from. Humbly reach out to this coach and ask for pointers. One of the leading aspects of receiving advice from other coaches is that one will quickly learn to adjust different pieces of the athletic program in order to meet the specific needs of the athletes.

Coaches Perez and Rayle discussing race strategy

2

YOU GOT THE JOB – WHAT'S NEXT?

You are pumped because you have landed the "dream job" of coaching middle schoolers in the amazing sport of cross country or track and field. The reality is that it may or may not be your dream job, but it could turn out to be. It is during the first few days of obtaining the job that the weight of your responsibilities sinks in. What should you be doing in preparation for working with the athletes whose development has been entrusted to your care?

Talk with Your Athletic Directors

The athletic directors will have a wealth of knowledge, information, and understanding to help you navigate your initial experience with these teams. Ask the athletic directors specifically for guidance regarding what the athletic department expects out of you. You need to know things such as when and where your teams can practice, when and where your teams compete, school-based athletic team rules, what to do if an athlete sustains an injury, the school policy regarding the use of social media and web-based sites, and your responsibilities regarding facility maintenance. Your athletic directors will be more than happy to make sure you have all of the information you need.

Read the School's Athletic Handbook

The athletic handbook will make clear the established rules, regulations, and guidelines for student-athletes, parents and coaches. Also, request a copy of the national and state governing body rules and regulations, and become familiar with the contents. Make sure to learn the athletic handbook to the best of your ability because situations will arise where your knowledge will be tested. Keep in mind that athletic directors and principals have very little sympathy towards a coach who ignores the handbook contents.

Talk with Building Principals

The principals will provide an academic and school-wide perspective to coaching. Ask how the whole-school mission lends itself to athletics. Finally, you need to know the established rules for athletic participation including what curricular activities take precedence over your athletic activities, the process for approving parent volunteers, and the procedures for dismissing an athlete from the team.

Talk with Experienced Athletic Coaches at Your School

Veteran coaches with familiarity of coaching at the school will be able to provide detailed information and advice. Ask the veteran coaches questions similar to those you asked the athletic directors and principals. The experienced coaches will be able to enlighten you about the written expectations and also the unwritten rules that need to be followed in order to be successful as a middle school coach in your particular school.

Get to Know Your Facilities

Investigate all parts of the areas where your teams will be training and competing. Your knowledge of every inch of the facilities will be beneficial in training and competition supervision. Make sure to know if or when your teams will be sharing facilities with other teams. When sharing facilities, work out schedules with the other coaches. If sharing facilities with high school athletes, it is most prudent to devise a schedule with the high school coaches. If the middle and high school athletes happen to be using the facility at the same time, you need to have a coach present with the middle school athletes at all times. When middle and high school athletes share facilities at the same time, it is common for high school athletes to feel entitled to the training facility over the middle school athletes. Without a coach present, this entitlement could lead to some athlete-to-athlete conflicts.

Recruit Assistants

Middle school athletes vary dramatically in their height and weight, and they also vary in their level of physical conditioning. The more coaches you have, the lower the athlete-to-coach ratio will be. Having multiple assistant coaches affords more opportunities for the development of the athletes. A note of caution; recruit quality assistants who share your philosophy. If your assistants are not on the same page as you in terms of proper coaching, the assistants can end up being more of a liability than an asset. Talk with your athletic directors about individuals you are considering for assistant positions. Your athletic directors will have insight to the past behaviors and motivations of the individuals you are considering. More information about recruiting coaches can be found in the next chapter.

Gather Historical Data

Middle school athletes and their parents appreciate knowing who was there before them and where they rank in the program. The emphasis here is not on who's the best in one particular aspect, but rather where the athletes fall in a wide range of categories. Include information such as who was on the team, how many years they were on the team, total meets or events they were in, placings in individual meets, time and distance rankings, etc. The more historical data you push out to the athletes and their parents, the more your athletes and their parents will want to be a part of the data.

Create Team and Individual Goals

It may be cliché, but your athletes will live up to your expectations. I recommend you start with the whole-team goals, and then delve down into the individual specific goals. These aren't necessarily championship goals. The goals should include matters such as positive attitudes, leadership skills, and sportsmanship. Explain to the athletes how meeting their individual goals will lead to the entire team experiencing accomplishments. Although the competitive nature may kick in where you and the athletes will have a goal to win, if winning becomes your number one emphasis, your teams will more than likely suffer when winning doesn't occur. To avoid the costly mistake of emphasizing winning, accentuate individual and team improvement and make it a habit to announce all of the positive growth that occurs both individually and as a team.

Recruit Athletes

Middle schoolers want to be involved with an athletic program that promotes positive relationships, friends, and overall feelings of accomplishment. You must let middle schoolers know this is what you are about. For the parents of children entering the middle school, knowing you are there to ensure the safety of their child and also create a sense of positive belongingness will make promoting your program an easy task.

When recruiting, if school policy allows, use social media and websites to publish information about the team. Include pictures of and stories about your athletes. Many times you will be able to add an athlete to the team because her sister, cousin, neighbor, etc. was a part of the team. Seeing these pictures and hearing the stories about the individual athletes elicits the "I want to be a part of this" reaction.

Establish a Preseason Conditioning Schedule

Middle school athletes love to be constantly engaged in activities. If you are coaching at a middle school where athlete contact is permissible prior to the start of the season, make it a priority to develop a preseason conditioning program that will be enjoyable and rewarding for the athletes. Plan with your assistant coaches who will be working with what events on what days and at what time. As you set up the trainings, mix it up with whole-team fun activities such as relays that will allow the athletes to physically develop while building team dynamics.

Distance runners enjoying preseason conditioning on a snowy day

3

ASSISTANT COACHES, VOLUNTEERS, AND PARENTS

The more eyes you have upon the kids, the more you will be able to see. The more you are able to see, the more you are able to help individual athletes make improvements and feel like they are part of the big picture.

The old adage of "too many cooks spoil the broth" does not apply to coaching middle school cross country and track and field. The point here is to get as much quality help as possible.

Athletes in this age group will range in abilities from beginners who have never run or picked up a shot put or discus to totally established All-Americans who flawlessly complete every drill. One trait I recommend you have in order to meet the needs of your athletes is the ability to delegate responsibilities. Recruit assistants, volunteers, and parents to take on roles that will afford you the opportunity to have multiple coaches spending time with the beginning, emerging, and established athletes. The more individual coaches you have directing the athletes, the more likely the athletes are to make gains throughout the season, not only in athletic abilities, but also in belongingness and self-esteem.

When recruiting others to help, look for quality and not necessarily quantity. Consider individuals who possess the same positive philosophy as you, possess a willingness to learn coaching techniques or who have complimentary traits you need in order to develop middle school athletes. Advice from veteran quality coaches is to keep the know-it-alls and win-at-all-costs volunteers and parents away from working with your athletes because the negative attitudes they bring to the table will have the ability to destroy all the positives.

Assistant Coaches

When looking for assistant coaches, talk with your athletic directors, principal, and veteran coaches about individuals who may be interested in helping you build the team atmosphere. There may be interested individuals who can free up their schedules one, two, or three days per week. There may be others interested in coaching who have the ability to free up their schedules every day they are needed. Find out if you have paid positions available or if the assistants will be strictly volunteers. You need to know the parameters under which your assistants can operate. For example, are assistant coaches required to undergo criminal history checks? Can the assistants be left alone for total supervision of the athletes? Can assistants ride on school buses, drive the school vans, etc.? This information must be shared upfront when recruiting coaches.

North Clay Middle School Cross Country Coaches

Volunteers

When recruiting volunteers, it will become evident that there are many individuals who are eager to help out in any way they can. Think of volunteers for day-to-day matters such as filling water bottles or placing hurdles on the track. They can also be responsible for event-specific expertise such as how to use starting blocks, or sporadic items such as timing or scoring meets. If a volunteer asks, "Is there anything I can do?" Your answer should be an immediate "Yes."

It is crucial to know the parameters under which your volunteers can operate, just as you will with your assistant coaches. For example, are volunteers required to undergo criminal history checks? Can the volunteers be left alone for total supervision of the athletes, ride on school buses, drive the school vans, etc.? This information will need to be shared up front when recruiting volunteers to help you with coaching your team.

Parents

When recruiting individuals to help, the greatest assets you have are the parents of your athletes. It is common for parents to fill the roles of assistant coaches and volunteers. The parents who attend every practice and every competition are great candidates and are frequently willing to help out in any way. Don't hesitate to ask parents for advice about fulfilling any need your team has. The parents of your athletes will either quickly take care of the need or have resources or connections to help take care of the need. Once your core group of parents becomes comfortable with you as a coach, many more will volunteer to help any way they can.

Parents leading team prayer

4

RECRUITING ATHLETES

Sell, sell, sell! Referring back to Chapter 1, middle school students are in a transitional period of their school lives, and many will be seeking ways to belong and build their esteem. With a coach who emphasizes a positive team culture and the development of abilities over winning, athletics becomes an avenue that allows equal opportunity for all students to meet these needs. The athletes involved in a positive program with an uplifting coach will be telling their friends about the enjoyable activities taking place. The positive approach will be an enormous asset in recruiting new athletes.

When recruiting, emphasize the wonderful aspects of cross country and track and field. Showcase the team atmosphere of cross country. Focus on the aspects of cross country and track and field that will draw future athletes in. Specifically stress how every athlete will develop his or her talents in a nurturing team environment. While recruiting athletes, think and act in a way you would want your child's coach to act toward your own child.

If you are taking the correct approach in your philosophy, you will be able to focus on the athlete's needs to belong and feel respected by stressing that every athlete gets to be a part of the action and every athlete has the opportunity to improve. This needs to be a prioritized selling point because middle school students desire to fit in and be accepted.

Create promotional flyers and videos. Include pictures and videos of your current athletes smiling, having fun, enjoying themselves, etc. Include pictures of practices, meets, team dinners, and any activity showing many athletes. Publish these flyers and videos everywhere you can, including the school website, Facebook, and team webpages. Ask the middle school principal and also the principals of the feeder elementary schools to hand the flyers out to the students in the next incoming grade level. For example, if your middle school is a seventh and eighth grade building, ask the elementary principals to give a flyer to every sixth grade student.

Visit the elementary schools that feed into your middle school. Talk with the principals and get permission to spend five to ten minutes in the classrooms where students will be in the middle school the following year. Talk about the sports with compelling emotion. The students will listen to what you're saying but will really hear your attitude and passion. When speaking to the elementary students, hand out a recruiting flyer to each student. Make sure the flyer includes your contact information for the parents.

Place the video and flyers in the hands of the current middle school students as well. In addition, find a couple of teachers who are fans of the team. Ask these teachers to show your recruiting video in class and to keep a stack of recruiting flyers available for students. An example of a recruiting flyer can be seen on the page 20.

Excellent middle school recruits

What is Track & Field?

The Sport of Track & Field is a competitive team sport offered to students in grades 6 through 8 that takes place in the spring. Track and field is a sport that includes 15 events. In the Track Events, athletes compete by running. In the Field Events, athletes jump or throw. In NCMS Track & Field ALL athletes get to participate in the dual meets. There are no cuts, and there is no bench to sit on and watch while others play.

The NCMS philosophy:

- Everyone is important, unique, and contributes
- Striving for excellence is as worthy as achieving it
- Everyone can reach for their personal best
- We will have fun, train hard, and compete well
- We want to inspire the joy of Track & Field

North Clay Middle School Track & Field is for you! We encourage all ability levels to join the team. We have a place on the team for everyone.

When & Where

NCMS Track & Field will have winter conditioning beginning in February from 3:45 pm to 4:45 pm at North Clay or Northview. A schedule of dates and times will be texted to parents and handed out to athletes. Schedules will also posted on the team website. http://ncmsxc.weebly.com/

How to sign up

Parents, please sign up online http://ncmsxc.weebly.com/

or contact Coach Tim Rayle at raylet@clay.k12.in.us

Facebook = https://www.facebook.com/ncmsxc/

Text Alerts = https://www.remind.com/join/ncms-track

Track Events	Field Events
3200 Relay	High Jump
100/110 Hurdles	Long Jump
100 Dash	Shot Put
1600 Run	Discus
400 Relay	
400 Dash	
200 Hurdles	
800 Run	
200 Dash	
2400 Run	
1600 Relay	

5

PRE-SEASON CONDITIONING

Whether you are building a cross country or track and field program from the ground up or beginning your tenure as the head coach or director of a program already in place, you need to establish your parameters in order to get athletes involved. If your local and state governing bodies allow summer or winter conditioning, this is a great time to do so. When publicizing that you are ready to begin working with the athletes, emphasize the who, what, where, when and how. Here's an example of this:

- Who = Middle school athletes
- What = Preseason conditioning for track and field
- Where = At the middle school track
- When = Monday; Tuesday; Thursday from 2:30 – 3:30 on school days
- How = Sign up with Coach _____
- Other = Parents must sign the consent

allowing athletes to participate. In addition, athletes must have an official physical on file prior to athletic participation including preseason conditioning. See Coach _____ for the forms.

- Contact = Please include parent e-mails & phone #'s.

As you begin to work with middle school athletes, divide the participants into groups of beginning, emerging, and established athlete categories based upon their current fitness levels. The beginning athletes will have a very low fitness level, normally struggling with the lightest warm-up routine. Beginners should gradually make progress to the point of being established. The emerging athletes will have a slight to medium fitness level and will be able to manage the warm-up and stretching routines but may not be able to physically continue into the workout. The emerging athletes will also need to gradually progress to the point of being established. The established athletes will have a high fitness level, will breeze through the warm up and stretching routine, and will physically be able to handle the workout. When your recruiting efforts pay off and your team numbers increase, the bulk of your preseason focus will be focused on the beginning and emerging athletes since they will make up the majority of your team.

Middle school athletes are frequently motivated and want to please their coaches. The good news is for middle school coaches, at this level, even the youth-deficient coach can keep up with the beginners in pretty much all of the activities. If you happen to be super youth deficient, recruit a youngster to be your sidekick and delegate the demonstrating of techniques to him/her.

Runners improve by running, throwers improve by throwing, jumpers improve by jumping, etc. Every middle school athlete on your team is going to train during the season, so you should have no problem helping them reach their goals in season. But what about establishing improved fitness levels out of season so that they can experience greater improvements during the season? How do you get middle school athletes to train for cross country and track and field outside of the normal season?

In order to get middle school athletes to train out-of-season, the sports of cross country and track and field have to be enjoyable. As a coach of cross country or track and field at this level, you must keep in mind that many youth and middle school athletes have had negative experiences with running. Non-cross country and/or track and field coaches use running as a punishment for undesirable results occurring during practices or competitions. Instead of using running as a positive motivator for increasing fitness levels, coaches in many sports traditionally use running as a penalty. For example, in basketball if a player misses a free throw, everyone on the team has to run. In volleyball if a player misses a serve, everyone runs. In football if a player misses a tackle, everyone runs. The examples go on and on as these instances can be found in practically all sports.

A great way to counteract these previous negative experiences with running and to get kids excited about the sport is to institute a preseason conditioning schedule integrating at least one, but usually two or three days per week of physical fitness games. Experienced coaches know that Manic Mondays, Wacky Wednesdays, Fun Fridays, etc. are ingenious as middle school athletes will jump at the chance to compete in fun activities.

To make the use of physical fitness games as an effective way to motivate, separate the athletes into groups and have them compete in any type of activity you can dream up. Often the athletes will put in a great workout without even realizing they're doing it. Also, the athletes will be telling their friends about the enjoyable activities you are doing, which then assists in recruiting new athletes.

The following are a few of the favorite Manic Monday, Wacky Wednesday, and Fun Friday activities according to middle school cross country and track and field athletes:

- Water Balloon Relay – Teams compete by running and then throwing the water-filled balloon to their teammates.
- Dice Exercise or Running – The numbers rolled determine the exercise or the time of the run.
- Sponge Relay – Teams compete to fill up an empty bucket with water from a full bucket. The buckets are placed 25 to 100 meters apart.

- The Time is Right – Teams run to multiple spots on campus and do an exercise or activity. Prior to the start, the teams estimate the time it will take to complete all exercises and activities. No watches are allowed.

- Luck of the Draw – Athletes draw a card from a common deck of cards. Based upon the card drawn, the athletes will complete an exercise or running length predetermined by the coach.

- Ice Cream Run – Run to the local ice cream shop and purchase ice cream for the athletes.

- Paddleball, Baton, Hula Hoop, etc. Relay – Teams compete by doing each of these activities in sequence with a 25 to 50 meter run in between activities.

- Obstacle Medley Relay – Teams compete by running 10 meters and then doing an exercise. The medley consist of a total of 50 to 100 meters before the next athlete goes.

If creativity is not one of your strengths, one of the easiest ways to find games for cross country and track and field athletes is to do an Internet search. Another option is to contact the director of local youth sports programs, such as the YMCA. If you have a strong youth running program in your area, contact the director. The directors usually love imparting their passion and will be more than eager to share game ideas with you.

Workload Progression

During the pre-season, have your established athletes workout three to four times per week in a controlled environment and an additional two to three times per week on their own. Your beginning athletes will need developmental periods that allow for controlled progression. On the two to three days when you are not playing fitness games, the focus will need to be on developing improvement in the fitness levels or event-specific techniques of the athletes.

As the athletes progress from beginner to intermediate to established, the amount and duration of the workout activities will progressively increase. Using distance runners as an example, during week one of summer conditioning the beginners may have a total daily workload--including warm-up, workout, and cool-down–of 1,200 meters, the intermediates may be around 1,800 meters total, and the established runners may be around 3,000 meters total. During the sixth week the total daily workload--including warm-up, workout, and cool-down for beginners should have gradually increased to 2,400 meters, intermediates to 3,000 meters and established athletes to the 4,000 - meter range.

6

WARMING UP, COOLING DOWN, AND STRETCHING

The importance of warming up, cooling down, and stretching cannot be overstressed. As a coach, it is a must to have a detailed understanding of proper warm-ups, cool-downs, and stretches in order to help your athletes succeed and stay healthy. Middle school track coaches should know so much about warm-ups, cool-downs and stretches that they (the coaches) can describe it in a way that is simple for the middle school athlete to understand and accomplish.

Based on a commitment to helping young athletes find success, some of the top youth track and field and running programs in the United States have excellent webpages and videos available for coaches to learn from. For example, the New York Road Runners Club (http://www.nyrr.org/) has a series of free resources including videos to help coaches understand the importance and mechanics of warming up and stretching. Just like in the local youth programs, the directors of these top-notch national programs are characteristically more than willing to help coaches learn. Check their websites and look for a link on how to contact them.

Warming Up

There are plenty of studies focusing on warming up prior to physical exercise. A common opinion is that warming up properly increases blood flow and flexibility and reduces the risk of injuries.

Many coaches new to the sports of cross country and track and field mistakenly believe the warm-up is nothing more than a very easy jog or effortless calisthenics. While the warm-up should be simple, it needs to be purposeful. The warm-up also needs to be done consistently at practice sessions and at competitions. As a side note, athletes in this age group are inclined to try to impress their friends by being first to the finish the warm up. To keep this from occurring, emphasize with your athletes the real purpose and importance of a proper warm-up.

NCMS Girls heading to the start line after warming up and stretching

Stretching

A vital part of the warm-up and cool-down routine is the stretching procedure. Just like warming up and cooling down, it is understood that proper stretching prevents injuries and reduces muscle stiffness or soreness.

It is common practice for coaches to have their cross country and track and field athletes use dynamic or "active" stretches after warming up and prior to training or competing, and use static stretches after training or competing and cooling down.

In order to gain a strong understanding of stretches to employ, conduct a thorough *Google* and *YouTube* search for *Dynamic Stretches to be used with cross country and track and field athletes.* Information obtained within the search will enable you to learn how to properly perform the stretches and also allow you to design a routine specifically to fit the needs of the athletes in your program.

Here are a few examples of *dynamic* exercises that can be used in an area 25 to 50 meters in length prior to practice and competitions:

- Fast Feet – Keeping toes parallel to the ground, the athletes move forward raising the feet 1 to 2 inches off of the ground.

- High Knees – Take a step forward lifting the knee to a 90 degree angle with the toes pointed forward, feet parallel to the ground

- Butt Kicks – With knees in line with the body and not lifted, alternatingly bring the heels up toward the buttocks.

- High Skips – Jump off of one leg, driving the opposite thigh into a parallel position to the ground. Also drive the arm opposite of the thigh up so that the hand is at the forehead level.

- Lunge Walk – Take a step forward with one leg. Bend the knee of the forward leg and plant the foot flat on the ground while the trailing knee moves to an inch off of the ground. Hold for a couple of seconds and then come back up to a standing position. Repeat with the opposite leg.

- Squat – The feet should be wider than shoulder-width apart. Move into a sitting position and touch the ground with both hands.

- Straight legs – Walking forward, keep one leg straight and raise it parallel to the ground as the opposite hand touches the toe. Repeat with the other leg.

- Cariocas – Move sideways, using the lead foot to push off and then crossing it behind the trail leg.

- High Knee Pull-ups – Slowly walk forward while pulling first one knee then the other up to the chest with both hands.

- Arm Scissors – In a standing position raise the arms so they are parallel to the ground. Scissor the arms alternating right hand over left hand.

- Hurdle Mobility – With the hands and knees on the ground and with the torso parallel to the ground, make a circular motion by lifting the knee and imitating crossing over a hurdle. Repeat in the opposite direction.

- Hip Rotation – While standing, lift the knee up so the thigh is parallel with the ground. Rotate the leg to the side and then back to the front. Repeat on the opposite side.

- Iron Cross – Lying flat on the back with arms stretched wide, rotate bringing the foot up to the opposite hand.

The following are examples of *static* stretches to use after practice sessions and competitions. Please note: If static stretches are used, the duration for holding each stretch should be for no more than 30 seconds.

- Arms & Shoulders: In a standing position with feet wider than shoulder width apart, place one arm across the chest and use the other arm to pull on the first arm.

- Hamstrings: In a sitting position, place one leg straight out. Bend the other leg and place the foot at the knee of the straight leg. Bend forward, keeping the back straight.

- Butterflies: In a sitting position, with the soles of the feet touching, lean forward while holding the toes.

- Upper Back: In a standing position, with feet wider than shoulder-width apart, lock fingers and move the hands away from the chest and then above the head.

- Lower Back – With the stomach and legs flat on the ground, slowly use the arms to push up the upper body.

- Abdominal – While standing, lift the arms above the head and gently lean to one side. Repeat, leaning to the opposite side.

- Pretzels – In a sitting position with the left leg straight and the right leg bent so the knee crosses over the straight leg, use the left elbow to push as the upper body is twisted to the left. Repeat on the opposite side.

- Ankles – While standing or sitting, lift one foot off of the ground and rotate the foot forwards and then backwards. Repeat with the opposite foot.

- IT Band: Lie on the back with one leg bent with the foot on the floor. Cross the opposite leg over the other leg. Hold on to the thigh of the leg that is on the floor. Pull toward the body.

Depending upon event-specific needs, make sure to slowly "warm up" the muscle groups needed for the specific events. For example, when working with an established group of mid-distance & distance runners, a 5 to 10 minute all-purpose warm up may be the warm-up of choice. In this example the runners start out with a 1 to 3 minute slow jog, followed by 1 minute of gradually moving into a sprint (pickups) with the last 10 to 20 seconds being close to an all-out effort. This is followed by another 1 to 3 minutes of slow to medium running and then another 1 minute of pickups. The last 1 to 2 minutes is a gradual return to a very slow pace.

When working with athletes in sprints, hurdles, and field events, caution is advised to make sure the muscle groups are properly warmed up prior to bursts of action. For example, when working with hurdlers, a 5 to 10 minute hip and knee flexibility routine may be the warm-up of choice. In this example, the hurdlers start out with a light 30 to 60 second run followed by a hip and knee dynamic routine including slow-to-moderate knee movements over a hurdle. This is repeated for 5 to 10 minutes. The key here once again is to make sure muscle groups are properly warmed up prior to the specific workout.

The following are specific-event warm up examples:

- Long Jump & High Jump: Start the warm-up with a very light jog of 2 to 4 minutes. Move into dynamic stretches that will focus on motion ranges and overall flexibility for jumping. Finally move into 5 to 10 minutes of drills such as 50-meter pickups focusing on the agility, speed, and strength needed for competition.

- Shot Put & Discus: Begin the warm up with a very light jog of 2 to 4 minutes. Move into dynamic stretches that will focus on range of motion for throwing, including arms, trunk, hips and legs. Finally, move into 5 to 10 minutes of event specific exercises.

- Hurdles: Begin the warm-up with a very light jog of 2 to 4 minutes. Move into dynamic stretches that will focus on range of motion for hurdling. Finally, move into 5 to 10 minutes of specific hurdle-mobility drills.

- 100 / 200 / 400 Meters: Begin the warm-up with a very light jog of 2 to 4 minutes. Move into dynamic stretches that will focus on range of motion for sprinting. Finally, move into 5 to 10 minutes of sprint specific drills, including starts.

- 800 / 1600 / 2400 / 3200 Meters: Begin the warm-up with 5 to 10 minutes of light jogging and light pickups. Move into dynamic stretches that will focus on range of motion for distance running.

- Cross Country: Begin the warm-up with 5 to 10 minutes of light jogging and light pickups. Move into dynamic stretches that will focus on range of motion for distance running.

Cooling Down

Just like the warm-up, the cool-down is an essential part of proper training and competition. Many times coaches and athletes at the middle school level believe that once the workout or competition is complete, the day is done. As a coach you must instill a routine of cooling down after practically every workout. The cool-down also needs to be very simple and allow for the muscles to properly "cool down." For example, with mid-distance and distance runners the cool-down can be 5 to 20 minutes of slow jogging, depending upon the race distance. When racing 3000 meters, a 1500-meter cool-down is recommended. Most of your athletes will complete this in around 10 minutes. When racing 800 meters, an 800-meter or 5-minute cool-down is advised.

It is important to note here that the recommendations are simply suggestions. As you develop as a coach you will create a prescribed cool-down and make adjustments in order to meet the individual needs of your athletes.

Big Hal after cooling down from a great race

7

WORKOUTS

How does a coach actually train middle school cross country and track and field athletes? One of the most complicated aspects of coaching at this level is developing workloads appropriate for middle school athletes. The one-size-fits-all approach is definitely not recommended because the physical maturation levels of middle school athletes are diverse. Athletes in this age range primarily benefit from the repetition of activity and becoming more familiar with performing movements. This need for repetitions is an excellent justification for emphasizing proper athletic form and technique with this group. Form and technique help a young person familiarize themselves with their ever-growing body, how their body works, and how best to control it.

Progressive Overload

Progressive overload can be applied to all athletes regardless of the event. Sprinters, hurdlers, distance runners, high jumpers, long jumpers, etc. can all benefit from this principle.

When using the premise of progressive overload, group your athletes into beginning, intermediate, and established clusters. You can even break the groups down further based upon fitness levels of the individuals within the groups. No matter the workout being prescribed, the basic idea is to slightly increase the workload, followed by appropriate rest, in order to create just enough stress for the athlete to adapt to the stressor and improve his/her performance.

Acquiring and Adapting Workouts

Specifically, what workouts are appropriate for middle school athletes? The answer will depend upon the age, maturation and ability level of the athletes. Appropriate workouts also depend upon the event an athlete is training for. The best resource for learning about appropriate workouts is coaches who have had continued success. State cross country and track and field associations normally hold clinics and conferences featuring successful coaches. The showcased coaches may provide workout examples for those attending the clinic or conference as part of their presentations. These coaches also provide contact information allowing attendees access to follow-up conversations. You should always take advantage of the opportunity to connect with these coaches and ask them for advice about workouts.

Internet searches can also provide great resources for creating appropriate workouts. Many top-performing programs, including those at the youth, middle school, high school, and collegiate levels, will post examples of the workouts they are using. While these cannot always be used without modification for your specific needs, they will provide you with an idea about what areas of concern go into creating and specifying workouts.

Another great resource can be found through bookstores. A normal search of "coaching track and field" will yield thousands of book titles. Within the books are hundreds of workouts that can be tailored to the needs of the athletes on your team.

Sample Workouts

The workouts presented on the following pages are for informative purposes only and are intended to introduce middle school cross country and track & field coaches to the concept of planning for an entire season. While the workouts listed are typical for the competitive phase of training, the workouts can be adjusted for the conditioning and recovery phases as well. When using the examples as a template for training, consideration should be given to modifying each workout in order to accommodate beginner, intermediate, and established athletes. The workout examples should also include a proper warm up, stretching, and a cool down. For more information on warming up and cooling down, refer to Chapter 6.

- Cross Country - Page 42
- Sprints - Page 51
- Mid-Distance - Page 60
- Distance - Page 69
- Hurdles - Page 78
- High Jump - Page 87
- Long Jump - Page 96
- Shot Put and Discus - Page 105

Key Concepts for Cross Country Training

- Standard middle school race length is 3,000 meters, which is approximately 1.9 miles.
- Periodization of training = (1) Conditioning Phase prior to the season starting; (2) Competitive Phase during the part of the season where athletes are racing against other teams; and (3) Active Recovery Phase while transitioning to the next conditioning phase.
- Stick to the model of workload progression discussed on page 28.
- Start the beginning of the season training slow and easy.
- Aerobic training = Slow running. Up to 90% of the energy used to run cross country races is produced aerobically.
- Anaerobic training = Fast running.
- Run minutes instead of miles.
- Teach proper running form, running tall and relaxed while looking straight ahead.

Sample Cross Country Workouts

Week 1	
Monday	5 minute warm up / active stretches / 15 minute group run / active and static stretches
Tuesday	5 minute warm up / active stretches / 20 minute group run / active and static stretches
Wednesday	5 minute warm up / active stretches /3 x 3 minute intervals at 3000 meter race pace with 5 minute rest between each run / 10 minute cool down / active and static stretches
Thursday	5 minute warm up / active stretches / 20 minute group run / active and static stretches
Friday	5 minute warm up / active stretches / 20 minute group run / team games / active and static stretches
Saturday	Off Day
Sunday	Off Day

Sample Cross Country Workouts

Week 2	
Monday	5 minute warm up / active stretches / 20 minute group run / active and static stretches
Tuesday	5 minute warm up / active stretches / 6 x 2 minute hill runs with jog back to start rest / 10 minute cool down / active and static stretches
Wednesday	5 minute warm up / active stretches / 20 minute group run / 10 minute cool down / active and static stretches
Thursday	5 minute warm up / active stretches / 20 minute group run / active and static stretches
Friday	5 minute warm up / active stretches / 20 minute group run / team games / active and static stretches
Saturday	Off Day or Competition
Sunday	Off Day

Sample Cross Country Workouts

Week 3	
Monday	5 minute warm up / active stretches / 25 minute group run / active and static stretches
Tuesday	5 minute warm up / active stretches / 3000 meter race or race simulation / 10 minute cool down / active and static stretches
Wednesday	5 minute warm up / active stretches / 25 minute group run / active and static stretches
Thursday	5 minute warm up / active stretches / 25 minute group run / active and static stretches
Friday	5 minute warm up / active stretches / 30 minutes of 1 minute race pace – 4 minutes slow pace / team games / active and static stretches
Saturday	5 minute warm up / active stretches / 3000 meter race or race simulation / 10 minute cool down / active and static stretches
Sunday	Off Day

Sample Cross Country Workouts

Week 4	
Monday	5 minute warm up / active stretches / 30 minute group run / active and static stretches
Tuesday	5 minute warm up / active stretches / 3000 meter race or race simulation / 10 minute cool down / active and static stretches
Wednesday	5 minute warm up / active stretches / 6 x 2 minute hill runs with jog back to start rest / 10 minute cool down / active and static stretches
Thursday	5 minute warm up / active stretches / 25 minute group run / active and static stretches
Friday	5 minute warm up / active stretches / 30 minutes of 1 minute race pace – 4 minutes slow pace/ team games / active and static stretches
Saturday	5 minute warm up / active stretches / 3000 meter race or race simulation / 10 minute cool down / active and static stretches
Sunday	Off Day

Sample Cross Country Workouts

Week 5	
Monday	5 minute warm up / active stretches / 30 minute group run / active and static stretches
Tuesday	5 minute warm up / active stretches / 3000 meter race or race simulation / 10 minute cool down / active and static stretches
Wednesday	5 minute warm up / active stretches / 3 x 3 minute at 300 meter race pace intervals with 5 minute rest between runs / 10 minute cool down / active and static stretches
Thursday	5 minute warm up / active stretches / 25 minute group run / active and static stretches
Friday	5 minute warm up / active stretches / 30 minutes of 1 minute race pace – 4 minutes recovery pace / team games / active and static stretches
Saturday	5 minute warm up / active stretches / 3000 meter race or race simulation / 10 minute cool down / active and static stretches
Sunday	Off Day

Sample Cross Country Workouts

Week 6	
Monday	5 minute warm up / active stretches / 30 minute group run / active and static stretches
Tuesday	5 minute warm up / active stretches / 3000 meter race or race simulation / 10 minute cool down / active and static stretches
Wednesday	5 minute warm up / active stretches / 30 minute group run / active and static stretches
Thursday	5 minute warm up / active stretches / 30 minute group run / active and static stretches
Friday	5 minute warm up / active stretches / 25 minutes of 1 minute race pace – 4 minutes slow pace / team games / active and static stretches
Saturday	5 minute warm up / active stretches / 3000 meter race or race simulation / 10 minute cool down / active and static stretches
Sunday	Off Day

Sample Cross Country Workouts

Week 7	
Monday	5 minute warm up / active stretches / 25 minute group run / active and static stretches
Tuesday	5 minute warm up / active stretches / 2 x 3 minute intervals with 4 minute rest / 10 minute cool down / active and static stretches
Wednesday	5 minute warm up / active stretches / 25 minute group run / active and static stretches
Thursday	5 minute warm up / active stretches / 25 minute group run / active and static stretches
Friday	5 minute warm up / active stretches / 20 minutes of 1 minute race pace – 4 minutes recovery pace / active and static stretches
Saturday	5 minute warm up / active stretches / 3000 meter race or race simulation / 10 minute cool down / active and static stretches
Sunday	Off Day

Sample Cross Country Workouts

Week 8	
Monday	5 minute warm up / active stretches / 15 minute group run / active and static stretches
Tuesday	5 minute warm up / active stretches / 15 minute group run / active and static stretches
Wednesday	5 minute warm up / active stretches / 20 minute group run / active and static stretches
Thursday	5 minute warm up / active stretches / 15 minute group run / active and static stretches
Friday	5 minute warm up / active stretches / 15 minutes of 1 minute race pace – 4 minute recovery pace / active and static stretches
Saturday	5 minute warm up / active stretches / 3000 meter race or race simulation / active and static stretches

Key Concepts for Sprint Training

- Sprinting is an anaerobic activity. Aerobic training is not sprinting.
- Focus on shorter workouts. Less is more when it comes to sprinting.
- Many sprinters also participate in field events, so moderate the training for all events.
- Guide and teach the athletes the technical skills such as proper form, foot strike, starting block technique, etc.
- Sprint mechanic walk = Emphasizing good running posture, the athletes walk focusing on staying on the forefront of the foot, lifting the knee to chest level with toes pointed up, and exaggerating the motion of the opposite arm by lifting the hand to face level. Right foot and left arm motion, left foot and right arm motion.
- Sprinter a-skip = Hands on hips, high knee lift, foot to knee level with toes pointed up, while skipping.

Sample Sprint Workouts

Week 1	
Monday	5 minute warm up with active stretches / 10 x 20 meter sprint mechanic walk / 10 x 20 meter sprinter a-skip / 2 x 100 meter sprint with walk back to start rest / active and static stretches
Tuesday	5 minute warm up with active stretches / 10 x 20 meter sprint mechanic walk / 10 x 20 meter sprinter a-skip / 800 meters of 100 meters running – 100 meters walking / active and static stretches
Wednesday	5minute warm up with active stretches / 100 meter sprint – 100 meters rest / 80 meter sprint – 80 meters rest / 60 meter sprint – 60 meters rest / 40 meter sprint – 40 meters rest / active and static stretches
Thursday	5 minute warm up with active stretches / 10 x 20 meter sprint mechanic walk / 10 x 20 meter sprinter a-skip / 6 x 30 meters starting from blocks / active and static stretches
Friday	5 minute warm up with active stretches / 4 x 80 meters with 80 meter walk recovery / 4 x 40 meter sprint with 40 meter walk recovery / team games / active and static stretches
Saturday	Off Day or Competition
Sunday	Off Day

Sample Sprint Workouts

Week 2	
Monday	5 minute warm up with active stretches / 10 x 20 meter sprint mechanic walk / 10 x 20 meter sprinter a-skip / 2 x 100 meter run with walk back to start rest / active and static stretches
Tuesday	5 minute warm up with active stretches / 10 x 20 meter sprint mechanic walk / 10 x 20 meter sprinter a-skip / 800 meters of 100 meters running – 100 meters walking / active and static stretches
Wednesday	5minute warm up with active stretches / 100 meter sprint – 100 meters rest / 80 meter sprint – 80 meters rest / 60 meter sprint – 60 meters rest / 40 meter sprint – 40 meters rest / active and static stretches
Thursday	5 minute warm up with active stretches / 10 x 20 meter sprint mechanic walk / 10 x 20 meter sprinter a-skip / 6 x 30 meters starting from blocks / active and static stretches
Friday	5 minute warm up with active stretches / 4 x 80 meters with 80 meter walk recovery / 4 x 40 meter sprint with 40 meter walk recovery / team games / active and static stretches
Saturday	Off Day or Competition
Sunday	Off Day

Sample Sprint Workouts

Week 3	
Monday	5 minute warm up with active stretches / 10 x 20 meter sprint mechanic walk / 10 x 20 meter sprinter a-skip / 4 x 70 meter sprint with walk back to start rest / 2 x 150 meter run with walk back to start rest / active and static stretches
Tuesday	5 minute warm up with active stretches / 800 meters of 50 meters running – 100 meters walking / 2 x 150 meter run with walk back to start recovery / active and static stretches
Wednesday	5 minute warm up with active stretches / 70 meter sprint – 70 meters rest / 60 meter sprint – 60 meters rest / 50 meter sprint – 50 meters rest / 40 meter sprint – 40 meters rest / active and static stretches
Thursday	5 minute warm up with active stretches / 10 x 20 meter sprint mechanic walk / 10 x 20 meter sprinter a-skip / 6 x 30 meters starting from blocks / active and static stretches
Friday	5 minute warm up with active stretches / 4 x 70 meter sprint with 70 meter walk recovery / team games / active and static stretches
Saturday	Off Day or Competition
Sunday	Off Day

Sample Sprint Workouts

Week 4	
Monday	5 minute warm up with active stretches / 10 x 20 meter sprint mechanic walk / 4 x 70 meter sprint with walk back to start rest / 2 x 150 meter run with walk back to start rest / active and static stretches
Tuesday	5 minute warm up with active stretches / 800 meters of 50 meters running – 100 meters walking / 2 x 150 meter run with walk back to start recovery / active and static stretches
Wednesday	5 minute warm up with active stretches / 10 x 20 meter sprint mechanic walk / 70 meter sprint – 70 meters rest / 60 meter sprint – 60 meters rest / 50 meter sprint – 50 meters rest / 40 meter sprint – 40 meters rest / active and static stretches
Thursday	5 minute warm up with active stretches / 10 x 20 meter sprint mechanic walk / 6 x 30 meters starting from blocks / active and static stretches
Friday	5 minute warm up with active stretches / 4 x 70 meter sprint with 70 meter walk recovery / team games / active and static stretches
Saturday	Off Day or Competition
Sunday	Off Day

Sample Sprint Workouts

Week 5	
Monday	5 minute warm up with active stretches / 10 x 20 meter sprint mechanic walk / 4 x 100 meter sprint with walk back to start rest / 2 x 200 meter run with walk back to start rest / active and static stretches
Tuesday	5 minute warm up with active stretches / 600 meters of 100 meters running – 100 meters walking / 2 x 200 meter run with 200 meter walk recovery / 2 x 100 meter run / active and static stretches
Wednesday	5 minute warm up with active stretches / 10 x 20 meter sprint mechanic walk / 100 meter sprint – 100 meters rest / 80 meter sprint – 80 meters rest / 60 meter sprint – 60 meters rest / 40 meter sprint – 40 meters rest / active and static stretches
Thursday	5 minute warm up with active stretches / 10 x 20 meter sprint mechanic walk / 6 x 50 meters starting from blocks / active and static stretches
Friday	5 minute warm up with active stretches / 2 x 100 meter jog / 4 x 70 meter sprint with 70 meter walk recovery / team games / active and static stretches
Saturday	Off Day or Competition
Sunday	Off Day

Sample Sprint Workouts

Week 6	
Monday	5 minute warm up with active stretches / 10 x 20 meter sprint mechanic walk / 4 x 100 meter sprint with walk back to start rest / 2 x 200 meter run with walk back to start rest / active and static stretches
Tuesday	5 minute warm up with active stretches / 800 meters of 100 meters running – 100 meters walking / 2 x 200 meter run / 2 x 100 meter run / active and static stretches
Wednesday	5 minute warm up with active stretches / 10 x 20 meter sprint mechanic walk / 100 meter sprint – 100 meters rest / 80 meter sprint – 80 meters rest / 60 meter sprint – 60 meters rest / 40 meter sprint – 40 meters rest / active and static stretches
Thursday	5 minute warm up with active stretches / 10 x 20 meter sprint mechanic walk / 6 x 50 meters starting from blocks / active and static stretches
Friday	5 minute warm up with active stretches / 4 x 100 meter jog / 2 x 70 meter sprint with 70 meter walk recovery / team games / active and static stretches
Saturday	Off Day or Competition
Sunday	Off Day

Sample Sprint Workouts

Week 7	
Monday	5 minute warm up with active stretches / 10 x 20 meter sprint mechanic walk / 4 x 80 meter sprint with walk back to start rest / 2 x 200 meter run with walk back to start rest / active and static stretches
Tuesday	5 minute warm up with active stretches / 400 meters of 100 meters running – 100 meters walking / 2 x 200 meter run / 2 x 100 meter run / active and static stretches
Wednesday	5 minute warm up with active stretches / 10 x 20 meter sprint mechanic walk / 100 meter sprint – 100 meters rest / 80 meter sprint – 80 meters rest / 60 meter sprint – 60 meters rest / 40 meter sprint – 40 meters rest / active and static stretches
Thursday	5 minute warm up with active stretches / 10 x 20 meter sprint mechanic walk / 6 x 50 meters starting from blocks / active and static stretches
Friday	5 minute warm up with active stretches / 2 x 100 meter jog / 2 x 70 meter sprint with 70 meter walk recovery / active and static stretches
Saturday	Off Day or Competition
Sunday	Off Day

Sample Sprint Workouts

Week 8	
Monday	5 minute warm up with active stretches / 2 x 50 meter sprint with walk back to start rest / 2 x 100 meter run with walk back to start rest / active and static stretches
Tuesday	5 minute warm up with active stretches / 10 x 20 meter sprint mechanic walk / 600 meters of 100 meters running – 100 meters walking / 2 x 200 meter run / 2 x 100 meter run / active and static stretches
Wednesday	5 minute warm up with active stretches / 100 meter sprint – 100 meters rest / 80 meter sprint – 80 meters rest / 60 meter sprint – 60 meters rest / 40 meter sprint – 40 meters rest / active and static stretches
Thursday	5 minute warm up with active stretches / 10 x 20 meter sprint mechanic walk / 6 x 50 meters starting from blocks / active and static stretches
Friday	5 minute warm up with active stretches / 4 x 100 meter jog / 4 x 70 meter sprint with 70 meter walk recovery / active and static stretches
Saturday	Off Day or Competition
Sunday	Off Day

Key Concepts for Mid-Distance Training

- Stick to the model of progressive overload.
- Mid-distance focuses on the combination of aerobic and anaerobic training.
- Aerobic training = Slow running utilizing oxygen.
- Anaerobic training = Fast running beyond the aerobic capability.
- 400 meter and 800 meter training will have a focus on 85% to 95% anaerobic systems.
- 1600 meter training will have a focus on 55% to 65% aerobic systems.
- Interval training = Repeated sequences of fast running at anaerobic threshold pace followed by a cycle of rest.
- Intensity = Percent of the athlete's current ability. An 800 meter runner with a 3:00 personal best working at 75% intensity would run 3:45 per 800 meters (75% of 3:00 = 3 x 1.25)
- Teach proper running technique emphasizing shorter stride length and slight forward lean of the hips.

Sample Mid-Distance Workouts

Week 1	
Monday	5 minute warm up / active stretches / 20 minute run / active and static stretches
Tuesday	5 minute warm up / active stretches / 4 x 1:30 intervals at anaerobic threshold pace with 3 minute rest between / 10 minute cool down / active and static stretches
Wednesday	5 minute warm up / active stretches / 25 minute run / active and static stretches
Thursday	5 minute warm up / active stretches / 4 x 3 minute intervals at anaerobic threshold pace with 2:00 rest / 10 minute cool down / active and static stretches
Friday	5 minute warm up / active stretches / 20 minute run / team games / active and static stretches
Saturday	5 minute warm up / active stretches / 3 x 2 minute intervals / 10 minute cool down / active and static stretches
Sunday	Off Day

Sample Mid-Distance Workouts

Week 2	
Monday	5 minute warm up / active stretches / 20 minute run / active and static stretches
Tuesday	5 minute warm up / active stretches / 20 minute run / active and static stretches
Wednesday	5 minute warm up / active stretches / 4 x 3 minute intervals with 2:00 rest / 10 minute cool down / active and static stretches
Thursday	5 minute warm up / active stretches / 20 minute run / active and static stretches
Friday	5 minute warm up / active stretches / 20 minute run / team games / active and static stretches
Saturday	Off Day or Competition
Sunday	Off Day

Sample Mid-Distance Workouts

Week 3	
Monday	5 minute warm up / active stretches / 4 x 200 meters / 10 minute cool down / active and static stretches
Tuesday	5 minute warm up / active stretches / 3 x 600 meters / 10 minute cool down / active and static stretches
Wednesday	5 minute warm up / active stretches / 25 minute run / active and static stretches
Thursday	5 minute warm up / active stretches / 4 x 400 meters / 5 minute walk rest between runs / 10 minute cool down / active and static stretches
Friday	5 minute warm up / active stretches / 200 meters with 5 minute rest / 400 meters with 5 minute rest / team games / active and static stretches
Saturday	Off Day or Competition
Sunday	Off Day

Sample Mid-Distance Workouts

Week 4	
Monday	5 minute warm up / active stretches / 5 x 200 meters with 200 meter walk rest / 10 minute cool down / active and static stretches
Tuesday	5 minute warm up / active stretches / 20 minute run / active and static stretches
Wednesday	5 minute warm up / active stretches / 1600 meters with 5 minute rest / 800 meters / 10 minute cool down / active and static stretches
Thursday	5 minute warm up / active stretches / 20 minute run / active and static stretches
Friday	5 minute warm up / active stretches / 3 x 300 meters with 300 meter walk rest / team games / active and static stretches
Saturday	Off Day or Competition
Sunday	Off Day

Sample Mid-Distance Workouts

Week 5	
Monday	5 minute warm up / active stretches / 5 x 200 meters with 200 meter walk rest / 10 minute cool down / active and static stretches
Tuesday	5 minute warm up / active stretches / 20 minute run / active and static stretches
Wednesday	5 minute warm up / active stretches / 1600 meters with 5 minute rest / 800 meters / 10 minute cool down / active and static stretches
Thursday	5 minute warm up / active stretches / 20 minute run / active and static stretches
Friday	5 minute warm up / active stretches / 3 x 300 meters with 300 meter walk rest / team games / active and static stretches
Saturday	Off Day or Competition
Sunday	Off Day

Sample Mid-Distance Workouts

Week 6	
Monday	5 minute warm up / active stretches / 5 x 200 meters with 200 meter walk rest / 10 minute cool down / active and static stretches
Tuesday	5 minute warm up / active stretches / 20 minute run / active and static stretches
Wednesday	5 minute warm up / active stretches / 3 x 200 meter pickups with 200 meter walk rest / 10 minute cool down / active and static stretches
Thursday	5 minute warm up / active stretches / 20 minute run / active and static stretches
Friday	5 minute warm up / active stretches / 3 x 300 meters with 5 minute walk rest / 10 minute cool down / team games / active and static stretches
Saturday	Off Day or Competition
Sunday	Off Day

Sample Mid-Distance Workouts

Week 7	
Monday	5 minute warm up / active stretches / 4 x 400 meters with 200 meter walk rest / 10 minute cool down / active and static stretches
Tuesday	5 minute warm up / active stretches / 20 minute group run / active and static stretches
Wednesday	5 minute warm up / active stretches / 4 x 3 minute intervals with 2:00 rest / 10 minute cool down / active and static stretches
Thursday	5 minute warm up / active stretches / 30 minute group run / active and static stretches
Friday	5 minute warm up / active stretches / 25 minute run / active and static stretches
Saturday	Off Day or Competition
Sunday	Off Day

Sample Mid-Distance Workouts

Week 8	
Monday	5 minute warm up / active stretches / 20 minute run / active and static stretches
Tuesday	5 minute warm up / active stretches / 20 minute run / active and static stretches
Wednesday	5 minute warm up / active stretches / 4 x 3 minute intervals with 2:00 rest / 10 minute cool down / active and static stretches
Thursday	5 minute warm up / active stretches / 20 minute run / active and static stretches
Friday	5 minute warm up / active stretches / 20 minute run / active and static stretches
Saturday	Off day or Competition
Sunday	Off Day

Key Concepts for Distance Training

- Stick to the model of progressive overload.
- Mid-distance focuses on the combination of aerobic and anaerobic training.
- Aerobic training = slow running. Up to 90% of the energy used to run distance races is produced aerobically.
- Aerobic pace = 70% of average mile pace. The aerobic pace of a runner with a 7:00 per mile average would be 10:00 (420 seconds divided by .70 = 600 seconds = 10:00 per mile pace).
- Anaerobic training = fast running.
- Anaerobic pace = 90% of average mile pace. The anaerobic pace of a runner with a 7:00 per mile average would be 7:46 (420 seconds divided by .90 = 467 seconds = 7:46 per mile pace).
- 2400 meter and 3200 meter training will have a focus on 75% to 85% aerobic systems.
- Run minutes instead of miles.
- Interval training = repeated sequences of fast running at anaerobic threshold pace followed by a cycle of rest.
- Teach proper running technique emphasizing shorter stride length and slight forward lean of the hips.

Sample Distance Workouts

Week 1	
Monday	5 minute warm up / active stretches / / 20 minute run / active and static stretches
Tuesday	5 minute warm up / active stretches / 30 minute run / active and static stretches
Wednesday	5 minute warm up / active stretches / 2 x 1600 meters with 3 minute rest between / 2 x 800 with 3 minute rest between / 10 minute cool down / active and static stretches
Thursday	5 minute warm up / active stretches / 30 minute run / active and static stretches
Friday	5 minute warm up / active stretches / 3 sets of 3 x 300 meters with 2 minute rest between each run and 5 minute rest between sets / team games / active and static stretches
Saturday	Off day or Competition
Sunday	Off Day

Sample Distance Workouts

Week 2	
Monday	5 minute warm up / active stretches / 20 minute run / active and static stretches
Tuesday	5 minute warm up / active stretches / 30 minute run / active and static stretches
Wednesday	5 minute warm up / active stretches / 4 x 3 minute intervals with 2:00 rest / 10 minute cool down / active and static stretches
Thursday	5 minute warm up / active stretches / 30 minute group run / active and static stretches
Friday	5 minute warm up / active stretches / 2 sets of 600 meters, 400 meters, 300 meters, 200 meters, 100 meters with 100 meter jog rest between runs and 5 minute rest between sets / team games / active and static stretches
Saturday	Off day or Competition
Sunday	Off Day

Sample Distance Workouts

Week 3	
Monday	5 minute warm up / active stretches / 20 minute run / active and static stretches
Tuesday	5 minute warm up / active stretches / 30 minute run / active and static stretches
Wednesday	5 minute warm up / active stretches / 2 x 1600 meters with 3 minute rest between / 2 x 800 with 3 minute rest between / 10 minute cool down / active and static stretches
Thursday	5 minute warm up / active stretches / 30 minute run / active and static stretches
Friday	5 minute warm up / active stretches / 2 sets of 600 meters, 400 meters, 300 meters, 200 meters, 100 meters with 100 meter jog rest between runs and 5 minute rest between sets / team games / active and static stretches
Saturday	Off day or Competition
Sunday	Off Day

Sample Distance Workouts

Week 4	
Monday	5 minute warm up / active stretches / 20 minute run / active and static stretches
Tuesday	5 minute warm up / active stretches / 30 minute run / active and static stretches
Wednesday	5 minute warm up / active stretches / 4 x 3 minute intervals with 2:00 rest / 10 minute cool down / active and static stretches
Thursday	5 minute warm up / active stretches / 30 minute run / active and static stretches
Friday	5 minute warm up / active stretches / 30 minute run / team games / active and static stretches
Saturday	Off day or Competition
Sunday	Off Day

Sample Distance Workouts

Week 5	
Monday	5 minute warm up / active stretches / 2 sets of 3 x 200 meters with 2 minute rest between runs and 5 minutes between sets / 10 minute cool down / active and static stretches
Tuesday	5 minute warm up / active stretches / 30 minute run / active and static stretches
Wednesday	5 minute warm up / active stretches / 4 x 3 minute intervals with 2:00 rest / 10 minute cool down / active and static stretches
Thursday	5 minute warm up / active stretches / 30 minute run / active and static stretches
Friday	5 minute warm up / active stretches / 30 minute run / team games / active and static stretches
Saturday	Off day or Competition
Sunday	Off Day

Sample Distance Workouts

Week 6	
Monday	5 minute warm up / active stretches / 30 minute run / active and static stretches
Tuesday	Warm up / Stretch / 3 x 1600 meters with 5 minute rest between runs / 10 minute cool down / active and static stretches
Wednesday	5 minute warm up / active stretches / 30 minute run / active and static stretches
Thursday	5 minute warm up / active stretches / 2 sets of 600 meters, 400 meters, 300 meters, 200 meters, 100 meters with 100 meter jog rest between runs and 5 minute rest between sets / 10 minute cool down / active and static stretches
Friday	5 minute warm up / active stretches / 30 minute run / team games / active and static stretches
Saturday	Off day or Competition
Sunday	Off Day

Sample Distance Workouts

Week 7	
Monday	5 minute warm up / active stretches / 25 minute run / active and static stretches
Tuesday	5 minute warm up / active stretches / 30 minute run / active and static stretches
Wednesday	5 minute warm up / active stretches / 4 x 600 meter intervals with 2:00 rest / 10 minute cool down / active and static stretches
Thursday	5 minute warm up / active stretches / 20 minute run / active and static stretches
Friday	5 minute warm up / active stretches / 20 minute run / active and static stretches
Saturday	Off day or Competition
Sunday	Off Day

Sample Distance Workouts

Week 8	
Monday	5 minute warm up / active stretches / 20 minute run / active and static stretches
Tuesday	5 minute warm up / active stretches / 25 minute run / active and static stretches
Wednesday	5 minute warm up / active stretches / 4 x 200 meter intervals with 2:00 rest / 10 minute cool down / active and static stretches
Thursday	5 minute warm up / active stretches / 20 minute run / active and static stretches
Friday	5 minute warm up / active stretches / 20 minute run / active and static stretches
Saturday	Off day or Competition
Sunday	Off Day

Key Concepts for Hurdle Training

- Walk through all drills with beginners until the athletes have a thorough understanding of each drill.
- Use mini hurdles when teaching beginners.
- Experiment with the start line to takeoff position going over the first hurdle.
- Focus on normal fast running with smooth hurdling.
- Lead leg = Leg going over the hurdle first.
- Trail leg = Leg going over the hurdle second.
- Strides between hurdles = Odd number of strides will result in the same lead leg every time. Even number of strides will result in changing lead legs.
- Lead leg wall drills = Stepping over the hurdle or cone placed directly in front of a wall or fence, leaning in and leading with the knee. The athlete's lead foot will strike the wall.
- Trail leg wall drills = Placing both hands on the wall or fence, with a hurdle placed in front of a wall or fence, leaning in raise the trail leg up to hip level, bent at the knee and pointing towards the hurdle. Swing the trail leg quickly over the hurdle in this position.
- Hurdle a-skip drills = On forefront of the feet alternating high knees while skipping.
- Hurdle b-skip drills = On forefront of the feet alternating high knees, kicking the foot out while skipping.

Sample Hurdle Workouts

Week 1	
Monday	5 minute warm up with active stretches / 10 x 20 meter sprint with walk back to start rest / 2 x 100 meter run with walk back to start rest / active and static stretches
Tuesday	5 minute warm up with active stretches / hurdle step drills /2 x starts with 3 sets of hurdles / active and static stretches
Wednesday	5minute warm up with active stretches / 100 meter sprint – 100 meters rest / 80 meter sprint – 80 meters rest / 60 meter sprint – 60 meters rest / 40 meter sprint – 40 meters rest / active and static stretches
Thursday	5 minute warm up with active stretches / hurdle wall drills / hurdle a-skip drills / hurdle b-skip drills / hurdle lead and trail leg drills / active and static stretches
Friday	5 minute warm up with active stretches / 4 x 80 meters with 80 meter walk recovery / 4 x 40 meter sprint with 40 meter walk recovery / team games / active and static stretches
Saturday	Off Day or Competition
Sunday	Off Day

Sample Hurdle Workouts

Week 2	
Monday	5 minute warm up with active stretches / 10 x 20 meter sprint with walk back to start rest / 2 x 100 meter run with walk back to start rest / active and static stretches
Tuesday	5 minute warm up with active stretches / hurdle step drills / 2 x starts with 3 sets of hurdles / active and static stretches
Wednesday	5minute warm up with active stretches / 100 meter sprint – 100 meters rest / 80 meter sprint – 80 meters rest / 60 meter sprint – 60 meters rest / 40 meter sprint – 40 meters rest / active and static stretches
Thursday	5 minute warm up with active stretches / hurdle wall drills / hurdle a-skip drills / hurdle b-skip drills / hurdle lead and trail leg drills / active and static stretches
Friday	5 minute warm up with active stretches / 4 x 80 meters with 80 meter walk recovery / 4 x 40 meter sprint with 40 meter walk recovery / team games / active and static stretches
Saturday	Off Day or Competition
Sunday	Off Day

Sample Hurdle Workouts

Week 3	
Monday	5 minute warm up with active stretches / 4 x 70 meter sprint with walk back to start rest / 2 x 150 meter run with walk back to start rest / active and static stretches
Tuesday	5 minute warm up with active stretches / hurdle step drills / 2 x starts with 5 sets of hurdles / active and static stretches
Wednesday	5 minute warm up with active stretches / 70 meter sprint – 70 meters rest / 60 meter sprint – 60 meters rest / 50 meter sprint – 50 meters rest / 40 meter sprint – 40 meters rest / active and static stretches
Thursday	5 minute warm up with active stretches / hurdle wall drills / hurdle a-skip drills / hurdle b-skip drills / hurdle lead and trail leg drills / active and static stretches
Friday	5 minute warm up with active stretches / 4 x 70 meter sprint with 70 meter walk recovery / team games / active and static stretches
Saturday	Off Day or Competition
Sunday	Off Day

Sample Hurdle Workouts

Week 4	
Monday	5 minute warm up with active stretches / 4 x 70 meter sprint with walk back to start rest / 2 x 150 meter run with walk back to start rest / active and static stretches
Tuesday	5 minute warm up with active stretches / hurdle straight leg drills / hurdle step drills / 2 x starts with 6 sets of hurdles / active and static stretches
Wednesday	5 minute warm up with active stretches / 70 meter sprint – 70 meters rest / 60 meter sprint – 60 meters rest / 50 meter sprint – 50 meters rest / 40 meter sprint – 40 meters rest / active and static stretches
Thursday	5 minute warm up with active stretches / hurdle wall drills / hurdle a-skip drills / hurdle b-skip drills / hurdle lead and trail leg drills / hurdle bounding drills / active and static stretches
Friday	5 minute warm up with active stretches / 4 x 70 meter sprint with 70 meter walk recovery / team games / active and static stretches
Saturday	Off Day or Competition
Sunday	Off Day

Sample Hurdle Workouts

Week 5	
Monday	5 minute warm up with active stretches / 4 x 100 meter sprint with walk back to start rest / 2 x 200 meter run with walk back to start rest / active and static stretches
Tuesday	5 minute warm up with active stretches / hurdle straight leg drills / hurdle step drills / 3 x starts with 7 sets of hurdles / active and static stretches
Wednesday	5 minute warm up with active stretches / 100 meter sprint – 100 meters rest / 80 meter sprint – 80 meters rest / 60 meter sprint – 60 meters rest / 40 meter sprint – 40 meters rest / active and static stretches
Thursday	5 minute warm up with active stretches / hurdle wall drills / hurdle a-skip drills / hurdle b-skip drills / hurdle lead and trail leg drills / hurdle bounding drills / active and static stretches
Friday	5 minute warm up with active stretches / 2 x 100 meter jog / 4 x 70 meter sprint with 70 meter walk recovery/ team games / active and static stretches
Saturday	Off Day or Competition
Sunday	Off Day

Sample Hurdle Workouts

Week 6	
Monday	5 minute warm up with active stretches / 4 x 100 meter sprint with walk back to start rest / 2 x 200 meter run with walk back to start rest / active and static stretches
Tuesday	5 minute warm up with active stretches / hurdle straight leg drills / hurdle step drills / 3 x starts with 7 sets of hurdles / active and static stretches
Wednesday	5 minute warm up with active stretches / 100 meter sprint – 100 meters rest / 80 meter sprint – 80 meters rest / 60 meter sprint – 60 meters rest / 40 meter sprint – 40 meters rest / active and static stretches
Thursday	5 minute warm up with active stretches / hurdle wall drills / hurdle a-skip drills / hurdle b-skip drills / hurdle lead and trail leg drills / hurdle bounding drills / active and static stretches
Friday	5 minute warm up with active stretches / 4 x 100 meter jog / 2 x 70 meter sprint with 70 meter walk recovery / team games / active and static stretches
Saturday	Off Day or Competition
Sunday	Off Day

Sample Hurdle Workouts

Week 7	
Monday	5 minute warm up with active stretches / 4 x 80 meter sprint with walk back to start rest / 2 x 200 meter run with walk back to start rest / active and static stretches
Tuesday	5 minute warm up with active stretches / hurdle straight leg drills / hurdle step drills / 3 x starts with 7 sets of hurdles / active and static stretches
Wednesday	5 minute warm up with active stretches / 100 meter sprint – 100 meters rest / 80 meter sprint – 80 meters rest / 60 meter sprint – 60 meters rest / 40 meter sprint – 40 meters rest / active and static stretches
Thursday	5 minute warm up with active stretches / hurdle wall drills / hurdle a-skip drills / hurdle b-skip drills / hurdle lead and trail leg drills / hurdle bounding drills / active and static stretches
Friday	5 minute warm up with active stretches / 2 x 100 meter jog / 2 x 70 meter sprint with 70 meter walk recovery / active and static stretches
Saturday	Off Day or Competition
Sunday	Off Day

Sample Hurdle Workouts

Week 8	
Monday	5 minute warm up with active stretches / 2 x 50 meter sprint with walk back to start rest / 2 x 100 meter run with walk back to start rest / active and static stretches
Tuesday	5 minute warm up with active stretches / hurdle straight leg drills / hurdle step drills / 3 x starts with 7 sets of hurdles / active and static stretches
Wednesday	5 minute warm up with active stretches / 100 meter sprint – 100 meters rest / 80 meter sprint – 80 meters rest / 60 meter sprint – 60 meters rest / 40 meter sprint – 40 meters rest / active and static stretches
Thursday	5 minute warm up with active stretches / hurdle wall drills with hurdle a-skip drills / hurdle b-skip drills / hurdle lead and trail leg drills / hurdle bounding drills / active and static stretches
Friday	5 minute warm up with active stretches / 4 x 100 meter jog / 4 x 70 meter sprint with 70 meter walk recovery / active and static stretches
Saturday	Off Day or Competition
Sunday	Off Day

Key Concepts for High Jump Training

- Guide and teach the athletes the technical skills.
- Use a bungee cord as the crossbar for training purposes so that the athletes are comfortable with the landing.
- Work on standing backflips into the high jump pit.
- Scissors kick drill = Take multiple steps and then scissor kick over the crossbar.
- Practice curved approaches utilizing multiple steps. Five steps directly in front of the pit and five steps to the right or left, depending upon the foot the athlete uses to push off.
- Drill proper takeoffs with lifting the dominant foot to knee level while the non-dominant foot pushes up.
- Practice clearing the crossbar (bungee cord).
- Step drills = Jumping, hoping, quick feet and butt kicks.
- Pop ups = Dominant foot planting and pushing up.
- Fosbury Flop = Distinctive style used to clear the crossbar when high jumping. The athlete runs in a curve towards the high jump pit, turns, and away from the cross bar and jumps over the crossbar back first.

Sample High Jump Workouts

Week 1	
Monday	5 minute warm up with active stretches / 10 x 20 meter sprint with walk back to start rest / 2 x 100 meter run with walk back to start rest / 5 x curve approach with pop ups / active and static stretches
Tuesday	5 minute warm up with active stretches / 2 x 20 meters of high jump step drills (5 steps then jump / bunny hops / fast feet / butt kicks / low bar approach with scissors kick) / active and static stretches
Wednesday	5minute warm up with active stretches / 100 meter sprint – 100 meters rest / 80 meter sprint – 80 meters rest / 60 meter sprint – 60 meters rest / 40 meter sprint – 40 meters rest / active and static stretches
Thursday	5 minute warm up with active stretches / 5 x straight approach / 5 x curve approach / 5 x low bar approach with scissors kick / active and static stretches
Friday	5 minute warm up with active stretches / 4 x 80 meters with 80 meter walk recovery / 4 x 40 meter sprint with 40 meter walk recovery / 5 x curve approach with pop ups / team games / active and static stretches
Saturday	Off Day or Competition
Sunday	Off Day

Sample High Jump Workouts

Week 2	
Monday	5 minute warm up with active stretches / 10 x 20 meter sprint with walk back to start rest / 2 x 100 meter run with walk back to start rest / 5 x curve approach with pop ups / active and static stretches
Tuesday	5 minute warm up with active stretches / 2 x 20 meters of high jump step drills (5 steps then jump / bunny hops / fast feet / butt kicks) / 5 x standing backflips on to the pit / 5 x low bar approach with scissors kick / active and static stretches
Wednesday	5minute warm up with active stretches / 100 meter sprint – 100 meters rest / 80 meter sprint – 80 meters rest / 60 meter sprint – 60 meters rest / 40 meter sprint – 40 meters rest / active and static stretches
Thursday	5 minute warm up with active stretches / 5 x straight approach / 5 x curve approach / 5 x low bar approach with scissors kick / active and static stretches
Friday	5 minute warm up with active stretches / 4 x 80 meters with 80 meter walk recovery / 4 x 40 meter sprint with 40 meter walk recovery / 5 x curve approach with pop ups / team games / active and static stretches
Saturday	Off Day or Competition
Sunday	Off Day

Sample High Jump Workouts

Week 3	
Monday	5 minute warm up / active stretches / 4 x 70 meter sprint with walk back to start rest / 2 x 150 meter run with walk back to start rest / 5 x curve approach with pop ups / active and static stretches
Tuesday	5 minute warm up with active stretches / 2 x 20 meters of high jump step drills (5 steps then jump / bunny hops / fast feet / butt kicks) / 5 x standing backflips on to the pit / 5 x low bar approach with scissors kick / active and static stretches
Wednesday	5 minute warm up / active stretches / 70 meter sprint – 70 meters rest / 60 meter sprint – 60 meters rest / 50 meter sprint – 50 meters rest / 40 meter sprint – 40 meters rest / active and static stretches
Thursday	5 minute warm up with active stretches / 5 x straight approach / 5 x curve approach / 5 x low bar approach with scissors kick / active and static stretches
Friday	5 minute warm up / active stretches / 4 x 70 meter sprint with 70 meter walk recovery /5 x curve approach with pop ups / team games / active and static stretches
Saturday	Off Day or Competition
Sunday	Off Day

Sample High Jump Workouts

Week 4	
Monday	5 minute warm up / active stretches / 4 x 70 meter sprint with walk back to start rest / 2 x 150 meter run with walk back to start rest / 5 x curve approach with pop ups / active and static stretches
Tuesday	5 minute warm up with active stretches / 2 x 20 meters of high jump step drills (5 steps then jump / bunny hops / fast feet / butt kicks) / 5 x standing backflips on to the pit / 5 x low bar approach with scissors kick / active and static stretches
Wednesday	5 minute warm up / active stretches / 70 meter sprint – 70 meters rest / 60 meter sprint – 60 meters rest / 50 meter sprint – 50 meters rest / 40 meter sprint – 40 meters rest / active and static stretches
Thursday	5 minute warm up with active stretches / 5 x 10 step approach / 5 x low bar approach with scissors kick / active and static stretches
Friday	5 minute warm up / active stretches / 4 x 70 meter sprint with 70 meter walk recovery / 5 x curve approach with pop ups / team games / active and static stretches
Saturday	Off Day or Competition
Sunday	Off Day

Sample High Jump Workouts

Week 5	
Monday	5 minute warm up / active stretches / 4 x 100 meter sprint with walk back to start rest / 2 x 200 meter run with walk back to start rest / 5 x curve approach with pop ups / active and static stretches
Tuesday	5 minute warm up with active stretches / hurdle straight leg drills / hurdle step drills / 3 x starts with 7 sets of hurdles / active and static stretches
Wednesday	5 minute warm up / active stretches / 100 meter sprint – 100 meters rest / 80 meter sprint – 80 meters rest / 60 meter sprint – 60 meters rest / 40 meter sprint – 40 meters rest / active and static stretches
Thursday	5 minute warm up with active stretches / 5 x 10 step curve approach / 5 x low bar approach with Fosbury Flop / active and static stretches
Friday	5 minute warm up / active stretches / 2 x 100 meter jog / 4 x 70 meter sprint with 70 meter walk recovery / 5 x curve approach with pop ups / team games / active and static stretches
Saturday	Off Day or Competition
Sunday	Off Day

Sample High Jump Workouts

Week 6	
Monday	5 minute warm up / active stretches / 4 x 100 meter sprint with walk back to start rest / 2 x 200 meter run with walk back to start rest / 5 x curve approach with pop ups / active and static stretches
Tuesday	5 minute warm up with active stretches / hurdle straight leg drills / hurdle step drills / 3 x starts with 7 sets of hurdles / active and static stretches
Wednesday	5 minute warm up / active stretches / 100 meter sprint – 100 meters rest / 80 meter sprint – 80 meters rest / 60 meter sprint – 60 meters rest / 40 meter sprint – 40 meters rest / active and static stretches
Thursday	5 minute warm up with active stretches / 5 x 10 step curve approach / 5 x low bar approach with scissors kick / active and static stretches
Friday	5 minute warm up / active stretches / 4 x 100 meter jog / 2 x 70 meter sprint with 70 meter walk recovery / 5 x curve approach with pop ups / team games / active and static stretches
Saturday	Off Day or Competition
Sunday	Off Day

Sample High Jump Workouts

Week 7	
Monday	5 minute warm up / active stretches / 4 x 80 meter sprint with walk back to start rest / 2 x 200 meter run with walk back to start rest / 5 x curve approach with pop ups / active and static stretches
Tuesday	5 minute warm up with active stretches / hurdle straight leg drills / hurdle step drills / 3 x starts with 7 sets of hurdles / active and static stretches
Wednesday	5 minute warm up / active stretches / 100 meter sprint – 100 meters rest / 80 meter sprint – 80 meters rest / 60 meter sprint – 60 meters rest / 40 meter sprint – 40 meters rest / active and static stretches
Thursday	5 minute warm up with active stretches / 5 x 10 step curve approach / 5 x low bar approach with scissors kick / active and static stretches
Friday	5 minute warm up / active stretches / 2 x 100 meter jog / 2 x 70 meter sprint with 70 meter walk recovery / 5 x curve approach with pop ups / active and static stretches
Saturday	Off Day or Competition
Sunday	Off Day

Sample High Jump Workouts

Week 8	
Monday	5 minute warm up / active stretches / 2 x 50 meter sprint with walk back to start rest / 2 x 100 meter run with walk back to start rest / 5 x curve approach with pop ups / active and static stretches
Tuesday	5 minute warm up with active stretches / 5 x straight approach / 5 x curve approach / 5 x low bar approach with scissors kick / active and static stretches
Wednesday	5 minute warm up / active stretches / 100 meter sprint – 100 meters rest / 80 meter sprint – 80 meters rest / 60 meter sprint – 60 meters rest / 40 meter sprint – 40 meters rest / active and static stretches
Thursday	5 minute warm up with active stretches / 5 x 10 step curve approach / 5 x low bar approach with scissors kick / active and static stretches
Friday	5 minute warm up / active stretches / 4 x 100 meter jog / 4 x 70 meter sprint with 70 meter walk recovery / 5 x curve approach with pop ups / active and static stretches
Saturday	Off Day or Competition
Sunday	Off Day

Key Concepts for Long Jump Training

- Guide and teach the athletes the technical skills.
- The athlete should be properly warmed up.
- Practice approaches focusing on maximum speed at the takeoff board.
- Approaches should be between 9 and 15 strides for beginners.
- Long jump step drills = High knees with toes pointed down during the plant and up during the lift, hops, fast feet, butt kicks, a-skip, b-skip, c-skip, and bounding.
- Practice standing long jump.
- Drive phase = Start of the running towards the takeoff board.
- Transition phase = Sprint posture with head up and accelerating.
- Sprint phase = Maximum speed with proper sprint technique.
- Takeoff phase = Launch foot pushing off of the takeoff board. Slight lean backwards keeping eyes focused straight ahead.

Sample Long Jump Workouts

Week 1	
Monday	5 minute warm up with active stretches / 10 x 20 meter sprint with walk back to start rest / 2 x 100 meter run with walk back to start rest / active and static stretches
Tuesday	5 minute warm up with active stretches / 2 x 20 meters of long jump step drills (high knees with toes pointed down during the plant and up during the lift / bunny hops / fast feet / butt kicks / a skip / b skip / c skip / bounding) / active and static stretches
Wednesday	5 minute warm up with active stretches / 100 meter sprint – 100 meters rest / 80 meter sprint – 80 meters rest / 60 meter sprint – 60 meters rest / 40 meter sprint – 40 meters rest / active and static stretches
Thursday	5 minute warm up with active stretches / 2 x 20 meters of long jump step drills (high knees with toes pointed down during the plant and up during the lift / bunny hops / fast feet / butt kicks / a-skip / b-skip / c-skip / bounding) / active and static stretches
Friday	5 minute warm up with active stretches / 4 x 80 meters with 80 meter walk recovery / 4 x 40 meter sprint with 40 meter walk recovery / team games / active and static stretches
Saturday	Off Day or Competition
Sunday	Off Day

Sample Long Jump Workouts

Week 2	
Monday	5 minute warm up with active stretches / 10 x 20 meter sprint with walk back to start rest / 2 x 100 meter run with walk back to start rest / active and static stretches
Tuesday	5 minute warm up with active stretches / 2 x 20 meters of long jump step drills (see week 1) active and static stretches
Wednesday	5 minute warm up with active stretches / 100 meter sprint – 100 meters rest / 80 meter sprint – 80 meters rest / 60 meter sprint – 60 meters rest / 40 meter sprint – 40 meters rest / active and static stretches
Thursday	5 minute warm up with active stretches / 2 x 20 meters of long jump step drills(see week 1) / active and static stretches
Friday	5 minute warm up with active stretches / 4 x 80 meters with 80 meter walk recovery / 4 x 40 meter sprint with 40 meter walk recovery / team games / active and static stretches
Saturday	Off Day or Competition
Sunday	Off Day

Sample Long Jump Workouts

Week 3	
Monday	5 minute warm up / active stretches / 4 x 70 meter sprint with walk back to start rest / 2 x 150 meter run with walk back to start rest / 4 x standing long jump / active and static stretches
Tuesday	5 minute warm up with active stretches / 2 x 20 meters of long jump step drills (see week 1) / active and static stretches
Wednesday	5 minute warm up / active stretches / 70 meter sprint – 70 meters rest / 60 meter sprint – 60 meters rest / 50 meter sprint – 50 meters rest / 40 meter sprint – 40 meters rest / 4 x standing long jump / active and static stretches
Thursday	5 minute warm up with active stretches / 2 x 20 meters of long jump step drills (see week 1) / 3 x 10 step long jump approach / active and static stretches
Friday	5 minute warm up / active stretches / 4 x 70 meter sprint with 70 meter walk recovery / 4 x standing long jump / team games / active and static stretches
Saturday	Off Day or Competition
Sunday	Off Day

Sample Long Jump Workouts

Week 4	
Monday	5 minute warm up / active stretches / 4 x 70 meter sprint with walk back to start rest / 2 x 150 meter run with walk back to start rest / 4 x standing long jump / active and static stretches
Tuesday	5 minute warm up with active stretches / 2 x 30 meters of long jump step drills (see week 1) / active and static stretches
Wednesday	5 minute warm up / active stretches / 70 meter sprint – 70 meters rest / 60 meter sprint – 60 meters rest / 50 meter sprint – 50 meters rest / 40 meter sprint – 40 meters rest / 4 x standing long jump / active and static stretches
Thursday	5 minute warm up with active stretches / 2 x 30 meters of long jump step drills (see week 1) /3 x 10 step long jump approach / active and static stretches
Friday	5 minute warm up / active stretches / 4 x 70 meter sprint with 70 meter walk recovery /4 x standing long jump / team games / active and static stretches
Saturday	Off Day or Competition
Sunday	Off Day

Sample Long Jump Workouts

Week 5	
Monday	5 minute warm up / active stretches / 4 x 100 meter sprint with walk back to start rest / 2 x 200 meter run with walk back to start rest / 3 x board jumps / active and static stretches
Tuesday	5 minute warm up with active stretches / 2 x 30 meters of long jump step drills (see week 1) / active and static stretches
Wednesday	5 minute warm up / active stretches / 70 meter sprint – 70 meters rest / 60 meter sprint – 60 meters rest / 50 meter sprint – 50 meters rest / 40 meter sprint – 40 meters rest / 3 x board jump / active and static stretches
Thursday	5 minute warm up with active stretches / 2 x 30 meters of long jump step drills (see week 1) / 3 x 10 step long jump approach / active and static stretches
Friday	5 minute warm up / active stretches / 2 x 100 meter jog / 4 x 70 meter sprint with 70 meter walk recovery / 7 approach repetitions / team games / active and static stretches
Saturday	Off Day or Competition
Sunday	Off Day

Sample Long Jump Workouts

Week 6	
Monday	5 minute warm up / active stretches / 4 x 100 meter sprint with walk back to start rest / 2 x 200 meter run with walk back to start rest / 3 x board jumps / active and static stretches
Tuesday	5 minute warm up with active stretches / 2 x 30 meters of long jump step drills (see week 1) / active and static stretches
Wednesday	5 minute warm up / active stretches / 100 meter sprint – 100 meters rest / 80 meter sprint – 80 meters rest / 60 meter sprint – 60 meters rest / 40 meter sprint – 40 meters rest / active and static stretches
Thursday	5 minute warm up with active stretches / 2 x 30 meters of long jump step drills (see week 1) / 3 x 10 step long jump approach / active and static stretches
Friday	5 minute warm up / active stretches / 4 x 100 meter jog / 2 x 70 meter sprint with 70 meter walk recovery / 7 approach repetitions / team games / active and static stretches
Saturday	Off Day or Competition
Sunday	Off Day

Sample Long Jump Workouts

Week 7	
Monday	5 minute warm up / active stretches / 4 x 80 meter sprint with walk back to start rest / 2 x 200 meter run with walk back to start rest / 3 x board jumps / active and static stretches
Tuesday	5 minute warm up with active stretches / 2 x 30 meters of long jump step drills (see week 1) / active and static stretches
Wednesday	5 minute warm up / active stretches / 100 meter sprint – 100 meters rest / 80 meter sprint – 80 meters rest / 60 meter sprint – 60 meters rest / 40 meter sprint – 40 meters rest / active and static stretches
Thursday	5 minute warm up with active stretches / 2 x 30 meters of long jump step drills (see week 1) / 3 x 10 step long jump approach / active and static stretches
Friday	5 minute warm up / active stretches / 2 x 100 meter jog / 2 x 70 meter sprint with 70 meter walk recovery / 5 approach repetitions / active and static stretches
Saturday	Off Day or Competition
Sunday	Off Day

Sample Long Jump Workouts

Week 8	
Monday	5 minute warm up / active stretches / 2 x 50 meter sprint with walk back to start rest / 2 x 100 meter run with walk back to start rest / 3 x board jumps / active and static stretches
Tuesday	5 minute warm up with active stretches / 2 x 30 meters of long jump step drills (see week 1) / active and static stretches
Wednesday	5 minute warm up / active stretches / 100 meter sprint – 100 meters rest / 80 meter sprint – 80 meters rest / 60 meter sprint – 60 meters rest / 40 meter sprint – 40 meters rest / active and static stretches
Thursday	5 minute warm up with active stretches / 2 x 30 meters of long jump step drills (see week 1) / 3 x 10 step long jump approach / active and static stretches
Friday	5 minute warm up / active stretches / 4 x 100 meter jog / 4 x 70 meter sprint with 70 meter walk recovery / 5 approach repetitions / active and static stretches
Saturday	Off Day or Competition
Sunday	Off Day

Key Concepts for Shot Put and Discus Training

- Guide and teach the athletes the technical skills such as proper posture, footwork and motion.
- Strength and power are connected with performance.
- The throwing rings are 360 degrees or 12 hours. The back of the ring is located at 0 degrees or 12 o'clock.
- Thrower exercises include active stretches of the quads and hamstrings, side lunges, carioca, butt kicks, high knees, high skips with arm circles, and running accelerations.
- Grip and placement = How and where the shot and discus are held.
- Shot put wrist flips = Flipping the shot put out of the throwers ring as if shooting a basketball free throw with one hand.
- Chest pass wrist flips = Two handed chest pass flipping both wrist out.
- Partner discus bowling pass = Athletes standing 15 feet apart, lightly bowl the discus to their partner.
- Power position = Facing the 90 degree angle from the back of the ring, the thrower's feet will be shoulder width apart. The athlete will bend the torso so the upper body and implement will be around the 0 degree mark.

Sample Shot Put and Discus Workouts

Week 1	
Monday	5 minute warm up with active stretches / 2 x 30 meters of thrower exercises (quads, hamstrings, side lunges, carioca, butt kicks, high knees, high skips with arm circles, accelerations) / grip and placement / active and static stretches
Tuesday	5 minute warm up with active stretches / 2 x 30 meters of thrower exercises (quads, hamstrings, side lunges, carioca, butt kicks, high knees, high skips with arm circles, accelerations) / grip and placement / active and static stretches
Wednesday	5 minute warm up with active stretches / 2 x 30 meters of thrower exercises (quads, hamstrings, side lunges, carioca, butt kicks, high knees, high skips with arm circles, accelerations) / grip and placement / active and static stretches
Thursday	5 minute warm up with active stretches / 2 x 30 meters of thrower exercises (quads, hamstrings, side lunges, carioca, butt kicks, high knees, high skips with arm circles, accelerations) / grip and placement / team games / active and static stretches
Friday	Off Day
Saturday	Off Day
Sunday	Off Day

Sample Shot Put and Discus Workouts

Week 2	
Monday	5 minute warm up with active stretches / 2 x 30 meters of thrower exercises (see week 1) / grip and placement / 10 x shot put wrist flips (arm extended above flipping the shot out with follow through) / 10 x chest pass wrist flips / active and static stretches
Tuesday	5 minute warm up with active stretches / 2 x 30 meters of thrower exercises (see week 1) / grip and placement / 10 x discus arm swings (feet shoulder width apart swinging the discus level with shoulders) / 10 x partner bowling pass / active and static stretches
Wednesday	5 minute warm up with active stretches / 2 x 30 meters of thrower exercises (see week 1) / 10 x shot put with bent knees, thrower moves hips forward and extends the arm while releasing the shot put / 10 x power position throws / active and static stretches
Thursday	5 minute warm up with active stretches / 2 x 30 meters of thrower exercises (see week 1) / grip and placement / 10 x discus arm swings (feet shoulder width apart swinging the discus level with shoulders) / 10 x partner bowling pass / team games / active and static stretches
Friday	Off Day
Saturday	Off Day
Sunday	Off Day

Sample Shot Put and Discus Workouts

Week 3	
Monday	5 minute warm up with active stretches / 2 x 30 meters of thrower exercises (see week 1) / 10 x shot put glide throws / 10 x shot put power throws / active and static stretches
Tuesday	5 minute warm up with active stretches / 2 x 30 meters of thrower exercises (see week 1) / 10 x kneeling throws / 10 x discus power position releases / active and static stretches
Wednesday	5 minute warm up with active stretches / 2 x 30 meters of thrower exercises (see week 1) / 10 x shot put glide throws / 10 x shot put power throws / active and static stretches
Thursday	5 minute warm up with active stretches / 2 x 30 meters of thrower exercises (see week 1) / 10 x kneeling throws / 10 x discus power position releases / team games / active and static stretches
Friday	Off Day
Saturday	Off Day or Competition
Sunday	Off Day

Sample Shot Put and Discus Workouts

Week 4	
Monday	5 minute warm up with active stretches / 2 x 30 meters of thrower exercises (see week 1) / 10 x shot put glide throws / 10 x shot put power throws / active and static stretches
Tuesday	5 minute warm up with active stretches / 2 x 30 meters of thrower exercises (see week 1) / 10 x discus arm swings / 10 x discus power position releases / 10 x 180 turns / active and static stretches
Wednesday	5 minute warm up with active stretches / 2 x 30 meters of thrower exercises (see week 1) / 10 x shot put glide throws / 10 x shot put power throws / active and static stretches
Thursday	5 minute warm up with active stretches / 2 x 30 meters of thrower exercises (see week 1) / 10 x discus arm swings / 10 x discus power position releases / 10 x 180 turns / team games / active and static stretches
Friday	Off Day
Saturday	Off Day or Competition
Sunday	Off Day

Sample Shot Put and Discus Workouts

Week 5	
Monday	5 minute warm up with active stretches / 2 x 30 meters of thrower exercises (see week 1) / 10 x shot put glide throws / 10 x shot put power throws / active and static stretches
Tuesday	5 minute warm up with active stretches / 2 x 30 meters of thrower exercises (see week 1) / 10 x discus arm swings / 10 x discus power position releases / 10 x 180 turns / 10 x 360 turns / active and static stretches
Wednesday	5 minute warm up with active stretches / 2 x 30 meters of thrower exercises (see week 1) / 10 x shot put glide throws / 10 x shot put power throws / active and static stretches
Thursday	5 minute warm up with active stretches / 2 x 30 meters of thrower exercises (see week 1) / 10 x discus arm swings / 10 x discus power position releases / 10 x 180 turns / 10 x 360 turns / team games / active and static stretches
Friday	Off Day
Saturday	Off Day or Competition
Sunday	Off Day

Sample Shot Put and Discus Workouts

Week 6	
Monday	5 minute warm up with active stretches / 2 x 30 meters of thrower exercises (see week 1) / 10 x shot put glide throws / 10 x shot put power throws / 10 x shot put 2-step drills / active and static stretches
Tuesday	5 minute warm up with active stretches / 2 x 30 meters of thrower exercises (see week 1) / 10 x discus arm swings / 10 x discus power position releases / 10 x 180 turns / 10 x 360 turns / active and static stretches
Wednesday	5 minute warm up with active stretches / 2 x 30 meters of thrower exercises (see week 1) / 10 x shot put glide throws / 10 x shot put power throws / 10 x shot put 2-step drills / active and static stretches
Thursday	5 minute warm up with active stretches / 2 x 30 meters of thrower exercises (see week 1) / 10 x discus arm swings / 10 x discus power position releases / 10 x 180 turns / 10 x 360 turns / team games / active and static stretches
Friday	Off Day
Saturday	Off Day or Competition
Sunday	Off Day

Sample Shot Put and Discus Workouts

Week 7	
Monday	5 minute warm up with active stretches / 2 x 30 meters of thrower exercises (see week 1) / 7 x shot put glide throws / 7 x shot put full throws / active and static stretches
Tuesday	5 minute warm up with active stretches / 2 x 30 meters of thrower exercises (see week 1) / 7 x discus arm swings / 7 x full throws / active and static stretches
Wednesday	5 minute warm up with active stretches / 2 x 30 meters of thrower exercises (see week 1) / 7 x shot put glide throws / 7 x shot put full throws / active and static stretches
Thursday	5 minute warm up with active stretches / 2 x 30 meters of thrower exercises (see week 1) / 7 x discus arm swings / 7 x full throws / active and static stretches
Friday	Off Day
Saturday	Off Day or Competition
Sunday	Off Day

Sample Shot Put and Discus Workouts

Week 8	
Monday	5 minute warm up with active stretches / 2 x 30 meters of thrower exercises (see week 1) / 5 x shot put glide throws / 5 x shot put full throws / active and static stretches
Tuesday	5 minute warm up with active stretches / 2 x 30 meters of thrower exercises (see week 1) / 5 x discus arm swings / 5 x full throws / active and static stretches
Wednesday	5 minute warm up with active stretches / 2 x 30 meters of thrower exercises (see week 1) / 5 x shot put glide throws / 5 x shot put full throws / active and static stretches
Thursday	5 minute warm up with active stretches / 2 x 30 meters of thrower exercises (see week 1) / 5 x discus arm swings / 5 x full throws / active and static stretches
Friday	Off Day
Saturday	Off Day or Competition
Sunday	Off Day

Skipper with an excellent shot put attempt

8

ORGANIZATION AND MANAGEMENT

The importance of being organized and communicating all aspects concerning your team cannot be overstressed. Prior to coming to middle school, students and parents during the elementary school years are informed about every decision that directly impacts the child. As a middle school coach, it is essential to keep these communication avenues open.

A middle school coach who is organized and communicates regularly with parents is not only able to stay on top of what is going on and when, but the coach will also gain tremendous support from the parents. Five of the most important areas to focus on are team behavioral expectations, attire and shoes, parent communication, practice organization, and meet organization.

Team Behavioral Expectations

In addition to communicating the school-based established rules, regulations, and guidelines for student-athletes, parents and coaches, it is wise to create a team specific code of conduct outlining the behavioral expectations and consequences for failure to follow the established team rules. It is advisable to have each athlete and their parents/guardians sign off that they have received a copy and agree to the code of conduct.

Attire and Shoes.

Middle school athletes and their parents will need to be informed about proper attire and shoes for training and competing. In many regions across the United States the weather during cross country and track and field seasons can change from one extreme to another. With weather in mind, make sure the athletes are wearing shirts, shorts and socks that help with pulling moisture away from the skin. The outer layers of clothing for cold weather conditions should include hats or headbands, moisture-wicking types of jackets and pants, and, if needed, sweatshirts and sweatpants.

When it comes to shoes for training and competing, middle school athletes tend to be impressed by the most flashy brands. Unfortunately the flash isn't always the best shoe for training or competing. Healthy muscles, tendons, joints, and bones can be maintained with the proper shoes. Recommend to the parents of your athletes that they research the most appropriate shoes for training and competition for their sons or daughters. It is advisable to visit stores who use experienced athletes as sales people. These experienced athletes will help the athletes with choosing the correct shoes with the appropriate fit.

Parent Communication

Communicate with parents as much information as possible. In middle school, there is no such thing as information overload. Schedules of practice and meet times and locations should be your first item to create and distribute. Team expectations, rules, and policies come next. Create a team list with parent e-mails, phone numbers, and emergency contacts. Keep this list confidential, but in your possession at all times in case of emergencies.

Subscribe to a texting service. Many are offered free of charge to school groups. Communicate via text all important information such as changes or cancellations, departure and arrival times, and directions to practices and meets. Parents and athletes also appreciate seeing the contest results immediately, so the text service can be used to post event results instantly after the event concludes.

Middle schoolers have a habit of leaving their belongings wherever they gather. Plan on having extra trash bags to collect their belongings wherever you happen to be. You can count on finding glasses, inhalers, computers, cell phones, books, articles of clothing, and the list goes on and on that your athletes have left behind. The parents of your athletes will appreciate a heads up every few days about the items you have recovered.

Practice Organization

Top-notch organizational skills are crucial for the success of individual athletes and the team. Be specific and down-to-the-minute. Practices need to include whole-team or event-specific discussion, warm-up, stretches, workout, cool-down, core training, etc. While the specifics of the prescribed workout sessions do not need to be published, the beginning and end times, drop off and pickup locations, and parent expectations need to be given to parents and athletes in advance.

Weather-related considerations need to be explained to the athletes and their parents. Always emphasize safety first. It is advisable to have a backup practice plan for those times when severe weather conditions occur. Stick to your plan and begin and finish on time.

Meet Organization

Meet organization includes course layouts, directions, workers, lineups, weather-related considerations, etc. Have your workers in place prior to the starting time of the event so when the other teams arrive you are able to have a smooth transition into starting the meet. Have opposing teams send you their lineups in advance. This will help with meet organization by allowing you to enter athletes into events and have electronic scoring. Entries submitted in advance create the ability for you to provide all coaches with a copy of the results prior to their departure from your competition facility. As a courtesy after the event, e-mail all visiting coaches and athletic directors an electronic copy of and a link to the results.

9

HOSTING A MEET

Hosting a meet at your home cross country course or track will provide an opportunity to display your organizational and management skills; feature your facilities; and allow your team, parents, and volunteers the occasion to highlight their talents. When it comes to hosting meets, this is your time to shine. Do all of the things that great coaches do. In no particular order, here are the basics you need to know in order for your home meets to run smoothly for all involved.

Entries

Prior to the day of the meet, have the coaches from the opposing teams submit their entries to you or someone you designate. Meet entries can be submitted in a variety of ways including but not limited to e-mail, Google Forms, a fee-based service provider, or through your website. When opposing coaches do not send their entries in on time, send friendly but firm reminders to the opposing coaches. Seek assistance from your athletic directors. Often the athletic directors will have positive working relationships with the athletic directors from the opposing schools. These relationships can be called upon to assist in receiving the meet entries.

Dual Meets

When hosting dual meets in cross country, unlimited entries are common. Check with your athletic directors for specific rules regarding entries. Regardless of the number of entries allowed, the rule of thumb is for seven runners to run varsity. Five of the seven runner's scores combine for calculating the team score. Whether the race is a varsity or junior varsity competition, the first five runners per team collect team points, and the sixth and seventh runners per team increase the opposing team's scores if placing in front of the other team's scorers.

When hosting dual meets in track and field, unlimited entries in each event are also common. In the varsity and junior varsity competition, two or three participants from the same school may score. It is conventional for the host school to run a separate varsity, junior varsity, and exhibition race in all of the track events with the exception of the distance races. In the distance events and field events, an unlimited number of athletes from each school may participate. The top two or three finishers from each school are allowed to score in the varsity and junior varsity competitions. The remaining competitors from each school will be considered as exhibition and will not score. Due to school conferences or leagues having different but similar rules, check with your athletic directors for the specific regulations.

Invitational Meets

Cross country and track and field invitational meets follow National Federation guidelines. In cross country, usually seven, but up to twelve, runners from the same school are classified and compete in the varsity competition. In track and field, two competitors from each school may be entered and compete in each event with the exception of the relays. Depending upon the host's rules, one or two relay teams per school may enter and compete in each relay event. Just as in cross country, due to school conferences or leagues having different but similar rules in track and field, verify with your athletic directors the specific regulations.

Contracts

If your school utilizes contracts when scheduling meets with opponents, confirm with your athletic directors that the contract is signed and the meet is on the school calendar. Your athletic director will contact the athletic directors from the opposing team(s) in order to verify the contract. Once the contract has been confirmed by all schools, you will want to begin the process of preparing for the meet.

Starter

Provide an official starter for your meets. State-certified and licensed starters have a working knowledge of cross country and track and field rules and will serve as the judge for all close finishes in the races. Having an official starter conducting your meets also drives home the point that middle school athletics is important and valued at your school.

Workers

Start planning early. Having enough workers covering all events and essential duties is crucial for the meet to run smoothly. Begin recruiting workers at least a month in advance of the date of the event. A group of individuals with basic understanding of the timing system is needed to time the races. A separate group of individuals with field event knowledge is needed to measure and record field event heights and distances. Curve or lane judges for the track races, and course judges for cross country meets are needed to supervise races and to report any infractions of rules to the starter.

The athletes on your team can be an excellent resource for helping out with non-essential duties. Train your track and field athletes to help with placing and removing the hurdles, uncovering and covering landing pads, and raking the long jump and shot put areas.

Equipment

Create a list of all the equipment needed to host the meet. Start with the basic equipment needs of your workers such as clipboards and pencils, starter's pistol, timing mechanisms, measuring tapes, and score cards. Next, make a list of the competition equipment needs of the athletes including shot put and discus implements, long jump markers and rakes, starting blocks, hurdles, and high jump and pole vault cross bars. Include basic medical equipment such as saline solution, bandages, and tape.

Communication

After your athletic directors have verified the

competition date, publish the information for the athletes, their parents, and other fans as soon as possible, giving plenty of advanced notice. This should be done on your team website, social media, via e-mail, text messages, and with paper copies being handed out to your athletes.

At least one week prior to the competition send a reminder to the coaches from the opposing schools. Include starting times, course layout, maps, parking instructions, restroom locations, and any other important information.

After the meet is complete, post results on your team website, on social media, and send a copy of a link to the results to the local newspapers along with the coaches and athletic directors from the opposing schools.

Course Layout and Maps
Create and make copies of your home course maps. Have these readily available for the coaches of the opposing teams and interested persons attending the meet. Post the maps on your team website and post the link to the website on your social media. Send the opposing coaches a copy of the map and the link to your website so they can share the information with the parents of the runners on their teams prior to the meet.

Place or Score Cards
In advance of the meet, make or purchase place cards for cross country, and score cards for track and field. The cross country place cards have numbers indicating the place the runner finished and are handed to the competitors at the end of the race in

the finish chute. The track and field score cards are event-specific cards with identifiable areas for filling in the runner's name, school, place, and mark. Score cards are filled out either at the finish line or at the field event by the finish judge you have designated at the events.

Timers and Scorekeepers

Once you have confirmation of your meet, recruit the help of timers and scorekeepers. The timers record finishing times and places. The score keepers record individual and team places and calculate and record team scores. If you are fortunate enough to have a fully automated timing system, the athletes competing in the event will be required to wear timing chips or bib numbers. If you don't have fully automated timing, in cross country, one or two timers will track the runners' finishing times by using either a stopwatch-printer or by marking times on a competition sheet. Once all the runners have finished the race, the timers relay the finishing times to the score keeper who matches the times with each runner's placing. The scorekeeper then tallies the team scores by hand or by using a computer-based program.

In track and field, up to eight timers will be needed to time and record each race. The timers are assigned a lane or a finishing position to time. One of the timers, or a separate individual, will serve as the finish judge who is responsible for recording the name, place, and time of all competitors in each race.

10

MARKETING YOUR PROGRAM

In order to influence kids, they have to know you are going to impact them. It's imperative to get the word out that your cross country and/or track and field program is a positive difference maker in the lives of middle school student-athletes. The old cliché is "either you tell your own story or someone else will," and it may not be anywhere near the truth. Cross country and track and field coaches are not known for their bragging abilities, so talking up your program will have to be learned. Rest assured, there are many avenues you may use to get the word out. Here are a few examples.

Parents

The parents of the current athletes will be your number-one resource. If you are organizing your cross country or track and field program properly and affording all of your athletes the opportunity for success, your parents will be telling their friends and other parents. This is another important reason to stay organized and to keep the parents of your athletes in the loop about all matters.

Social Media

There are two things middle school athletes have a passion about – pictures of their friends and pictures of themselves. More importantly, they love seeing these pictures on social media. Harness this energy to promote your teams. Three social media favorites are

- *Facebook* – This is a great resource for the parents, grandparents, teachers, and any others interested in your program. Post pictures, comments, and any other information necessary to instill a sense of pride in what is happening with and on your teams.

- *Instagram* – Many of your athletes and their parents will be followers of your teams on Instagram. While at practices and meets, post pictures of your athletes doing the things they enjoy. Make sure to include pictures of all of your athletes in order to emphasize that every athlete on the team is important. Also, come up with a unique hashtag for your team. For example, at the end of each post when you make comments, add a tag such as #NCMS XC Rocks! The great thing with Instagram is that you can link your Facebook and Twitter accounts so that your posts go directly to these. You don't have to repeatedly login to these accounts in order to replicate your posts.

- *Twitter* – As with Instagram, many of your athletes and their parents will follow your teams on Twitter. In addition, you'll find a base of like-minded coaches and athletes will follow your team. While at practices and meets, post pictures and include catchy phrases to draw your fans in. With Twitter, you'll also want to come up with a unique hashtag for your team.

Fellow Coaches and Sponsors

One of your greatest assets will be the other coaches of sports and sponsors of other activities within your school. Success breeds success, so promoting your program's success will only help to get others interested in the school and other programs. Many times the coaches and sponsors at your school will repost your Facebook, Instagram, and Twitter posts to their followers. This results in their followers becoming your followers, thus increasing the reach of your program.

Spirit Wear

Middle school athletes want to look good. This can come in handy as you promote your team through spirit wear. Get creative with the design. Much like a school logo, once you have a design that fits your team, make it your brand logo. You do not have to stick with your school colors for spirit wear. If the athletes want tie dye or neon colors, get the tie dye or neon. As your program grows, others outside of your team, such as the parents or friends of your athletes, will also request to order spirit wear. Make the items available for anyone wanting to support your program. When your team grows in number, so will the number of your fans. One of the trendy things about spirit wear is that your fans will attend meets and practices wearing your items.

Individual / Team Records

Your athletes will almost immediately want to know where they fall within the history of the program. Another way to market your program is to publish these records. Middle school students in physical education class may participate in cross country and track and field as part of the curriculum. If these students are aware of the records and see that they are beating or close to beating the marks, there is a good chance they will want to join the team.

Personal Record Cards

A great way to motivate athletes and get athletes interested in your program at the same time is by publishing your athletes' personal records (PRs). One way to do this is by creating personal record cards that contain the date of the meet, the event, the athlete's name, and the personal record achieved. In addition to posting the PR cards on your social media accounts, the cards can be printed and handed out during team meetings. The more celebrations around PRs, the more others will want to be involved with your program.

Nicknames

Another easy way to get athletes interested in your program is by assuring the athletes are getting individualized positive attention. A way to make certain the athletes feel they belong on the team is by giving each individual a unique nickname that compliments their personality. When done in a positive way, the athletes will naturally address each other at school and school-related activities by their nicknames. This will garner interest from individuals not on the team and provide you with another easy recruiting tool. Some examples of nicknames:

Big Hal	Crash
Pistol Pete	Spud
Boomer	Mighty B
Meggie	Dr. Pepper
Hostess	Corn
Hankinator	The Beast
Lil' Dawg	Junior
Triple L	Nicester
Captain America	Sandpiper
Orange Crush	Cupcake
Vlasic	Yappy
Shak	Sticks
Apple Jax	Spud
Rudy	Danny Ocean
Rooster	Dory
Lil' Sweet	Northern Lights

Corn, Sandpiper, Triple L, Big Hal, and Nicester

11

FINAL THOUGHTS

The biggest takeaways from working with middle school athletes will be the amazing experiences you get to be a part of, helping the student-athletes develop socially and athletically, and the memories of the athletes and teams that will last a lifetime for both the athletes and you. If approached from a standpoint of wanting to learn as much as teach, the time spent coaching will be incredible.

Middle school athletes are eager to please, but want to do so on their own terms. With this in mind, know that patience is definitely a virtue. If your focus is on the development of all of the athletes in your program regardless of ability and not on "winning at all costs," you and your athletes will excel.

Important Considerations

As a new coach, or a coach looking to improve, you will find many individuals willing to help you. The athletic directors at your school are your primary resource for matching you up with those individuals.

Once you have others to bounce ideas with, make a game plan and begin implementing your plan.

When working with middle school athletes, your focus must be on the athletic and social development of each of the athletes. Place your emphasis on helping each child in this process and not on the end product of winning.

I advise you never to put your center of attention on only the best athletes. As a middle school coach, never follow this terrible philosophy: "I only focus on my best athletes because my goal is to win." Instead, stick to a philosophy such as this: "I reinforce the positive attributes exhibited by each of my athletes because I believe in building a foundation for lifetime success."

Middle school athletes are in a transition period. Your shortest and least athletic middle schooler may become the tallest and most athletic high schooler. If you maintain an equal balance of paying attention to all of your athletes, you will increase the likelihood of the children experiencing success and continuing on in the sports.

Finally, keep in mind that the well-being of each athlete you are working with is of prime importance to the athlete's parents. By treating each child with dignity and respect, you will be fostering a positive relationship with both the child and the parents.

Reasonable Expectations

It is advisable not to try to implement every new idea you come across at once. Instead, evaluate your program and gradually apply bits and pieces of the concepts you would like to try out, adapting or modifying what you are currently doing. In doing so, you will be able to assess what works and what doesn't with the athletes you are coaching.

The Beast and Spud after a great race

ABOUT THE AUTHOR

Timothy Rayle began working with athletes as the middle school cross country coach at Eastside Jr/Sr High School in Butler, Indiana. After 15 years of successful coaching at the middle and high school levels he stepped away to pursue interests in educational leadership. In 2016 he returned to coaching cross country and track and field at North Clay Middle School in Brazil, Indiana. Throughout his career, the individual and total program successes are unmatched under his leadership, including the 2017 Indiana Middle School State Championship in girls cross country, and the 2019 Indiana Middle School State Championship in girls track and field.

Timothy Rayle with NCMS athlete Hannah

Made in the USA
Middletown, DE
09 September 2019